Prepare
Yourself

A Message To the Christian—
Why God's Judgment Is
Coming On America!

BOB FRALEY

Copyright © 1998
Revised 2003
Robert R. Fraley
All rights reserved
ISBN — 0-9612999-3-2

Published by
Christina Life Outreach
6438 East Jenan Drive
Scottsdale, Arizona 85254

Printed in the United States of America

Cover design and book layout by Paul Annan

Contents

Introduction

Before I share the message of this book I want to tell you something about my wife, Barbara, myself and our family so that you can become better acquainted with us.

Barbara and I were both raised in Christian homes, and we both accepted the Lord Jesus Christ as our personal Savior at a young age. I still remember being baptized in a muddy creek that wound through the small farm where I was raised in southwestern Ohio.

During the first seven and a half years of our marriage our commitment to serve the Lord was not what it should have been. Then in the fall of 1964 we were convicted at a revival meeting to recommit our hearts and lives to completely serve the Lord Jesus Christ.

We were very busy the first five years in serving the Lord. Barbara was known as "Mrs. Energy." The Lord put her boundless gift of hospitality, ability to cheer the heart, and minister comfort and peace in a heartwarming atmosphere to full use. We studied the Word of God, helped the elderly, the poor and needy, and I was able to teach and occasionally preach at church. Barbara would often have from 10 to 20 and sometimes up to 150 people at our house for dinner, recreational activities and Bible studies.

We were excited about our Bible studies and service. Serving the Lord, raising our two sons, serving in our church, helping neighbors and friends, along with my position as vice president and general manager of a manufacturing company were the center of our activities.

Then on October 4, 1969, an event happened that changed everything in our family life. Barbara and I had gone out of town that day. We had left our oldest son with our minister and his family. When we returned home late that evening, they told us that one of the elders from our church, along with his wife and three of their six children, had been in a terrible and tragic automobile accident. Both parents had been killed instantly.

Of the three children in the accident, the ten-year-old daughter, Andrea, had a fractured skull and such severe brain damage that hospital doctors pronounced her hopeless. The hospital staff didn't even clean her up from the accident. They decided to leave that job for the mortuary. Alice, four-years-old, was on the critical list but was expected to fully recover with no complications. Sixteen-year-old Larry had escaped with only minor cuts and bruises.

Over the next few days the Lord gave Barbara and me very clear direction that we were to take these six orphaned children whose parents were killed and raise them for Him.

Though we didn't think we had the time or know how, Barbara and I were obedient to that call from the Lord. I was 34 and Barbara was 31 years old at the time. The Word of God does promise that if He calls us to do a task for Him, He will provide us with whatever we need. Jesus said, **"You did not choose me, but I chose you and appointed you to go and**

bear fruit—fruit that will last. Then the Father will give you whatever you ask in my name" (John 15:16).

Our obedience to that call from the Lord, which will soon be 35 years ago, was the beginning of many miraculous things the Lord has done in our lives. It is impossible for me to share them in this brief testimony, but I would like to tell you about one.

Remember the ten-year-old daughter, Andrea, who was so critically injured in the accident that the doctors said there was no hope for her to survive? Christians began to pray for Andrea. She lived through the first night, so the next day she was transferred to a different hospital closer to home.

The attending physician at the new hospital said they would have to perform surgery to relieve the pressure on her brain for there to be any possibility of saving Andrea's life. He warned, however, that even if the procedure was successful and she lived, we should understand that Andrea would not be able to return to school until the following fall—eleven months away. Even then, she could never make a complete recovery but would be disabled, both physically and mentally, for life.

Barbara and I can testify, along with many others, that the Lord completely healed Andrea of the brain damage she received in the accident, and she was back in school within three weeks. The surgeons never had a chance to perform their operation.

Another beautiful thing happened when the Lord healed Andrea. From the time she was a baby, she had had a malfunctioning kidney. She took medicine twice a day for her kidney problem and had been under a doctor's care since birth. This kidney problem caused her to often be sick, and at ten years of age she only weighed 41 pounds.

The Lord's healing was complete. He also healed this malfunctioning kidney when He healed her injuries from the accident. Kidney medicine and frequent visits to the doctor became a thing of the past. Her weight doubled to 82 pounds within a year, and she changed from that of a frail, sickly child to a strong, robust child.

Today, Andrea and her husband have four boys and own and operate a large dairy farm near Phoenix, Arizona.

After taking in these children to raise, the Lord began a powerful spiritual work in the life of Barbara and me by teaching us about His ways from Scripture. Over the years we have received several warnings from the Lord about the tremendous spiritual warfare taking place in our country to destroy America's Christian heritage. These warnings have been of tremendous benefit in helping us build a strong spiritual ark for guiding our family's Christian walk in these troubled times. Our own three children (our youngest was born after taking in the other six children), and the six we took to raise plus the children's spouses and our nineteen grandchildren who are old enough, have all received the Lord Jesus Christ as their personal Savior.

Bob Fraley

AMERICA IN THE LAST DAYS

Prelude

God has had a very special place in His heart for America and the American people. The history of our nation confirms this to be a true fact.

America has been the world's center of Christianity for over 300 years. God has used our people and our resources to take the gospel of Jesus Christ throughout the world.

I will share with you a few highlights from the development of our country's spiritual history. I want you to particularly note that these are highlights from America's spiritual history, not our secular history. It is important to make a distinction between the two and not mix them together. Doing so has often caused confusion.

The major thrust of our country's spiritual history began with a group of committed Christians who were living in England. These Christians, who became known as the Pilgrims, were willing to sacrifice everything so they could find a place to worship God in freedom. They left their homes, jobs, possessions, friends and relatives and suffered many personal hardships to enjoy freedom of worship.

To fulfill that desire, 35 of these Christians ventured to a newly discovered land called America. They crossed the Atlantic Ocean in a ship called the "Mayflower" in the year 1607. The Pilgrims were the first people to bring the light of Christianity to America.

The next highlight in our country's spiritual development began about 20 years later. Over 20,000 Christians, called the Puritans, migrated to America from Europe between the years of 1628 to 1644. For population comparison that would be like 3,000,000 Americans packing up today and leaving.

The 1700s brought the powerfully anointed preaching of John and Charles Wesley, George Whitefield, David Brainerd, Jonathan Edwards and others during the "Great Awakening" revival that took place in our country. It was the preaching of these men that set the tone for our Constitution. Fifty-two out of the fifty-five original signers of the Declaration of Independence confessed a personal relationship with Jesus Christ as their Lord and Savior. That is why many of the original laws of our government were founded upon the teachings of the Bible. One of our founding fathers and 2nd president, John Adams, said, *"Our Constitution was made only for a moral and a religious people. It is wholly inadequate to the government of any other."* His son, John Quincy Adams, the 6th president stated, *"The highest glory of the American Revolution was this: It connected in one indissoluble bond, the principles of civil government with those of Christianity."*

Christians who were led by God to be salt and light settled our country. They did not let secular society form our way of government. Early Christians were involved in forming our Constitution, Bill of Rights, and in every other aspect of developing our Republic form of government. They were given wisdom and inspiration from God; no man had the wisdom and foresight it took to build America. The writings and quotes of our founding fathers were prophetic in nature, warning us of the exact problems we are facing today.

The next major event that took place in our country's spiritual history was between the years of 1800 and 1900, when thousands of churches were established throughout our land. Today a church is found every few blocks in most towns across this nation, and the gospel is preached every day in our country through every communication media available.

However, in the 1950s the storms of a major spiritual problem began to develop in our country. It seemed to begin after World War II—after we became the greatest superpower in the history of mankind. It is a problem that has continued to grow in this last generation, which has puzzled most Christians. The spiritual problem is this: how in this nation, which had such a strong Christian foundation and where so much Christian teaching has taken place, could our society be experiencing such a rapid increase in the spirit of lawlessness, permissiveness, rebellion and selfishness? A condition that has continued to get worse over the last 30 to 40 years and now has gotten completely out of control. And nothing—whether it is new programs, education, or anything else—seems to have much effect on changing what is happening.

Any American willing to face reality must admit that soon after World War II we spiritually began to experience a period of heavy spiritual warfare and it has continued to this day. It was soon after WW II that the moral standards which had bound our nation and our people together for centuries began to unravel. Even our government leaders began to pass legislation that allowed and promoted immoral causes and ungodly standards on issues they never before would have considered. Passing out condoms in schools, for example, sanctions promiscuity, which promotes sexual immorality. Prayer was made illegal in all public schools. A law was passed that has allowed the murder of over forty million human lives through abortion. These things didn't happen until we became "king of the hill" so to speak in world affairs.

In this generation we have changed the way we think, raise our families, run our public schools, run our government, set our moral standards, and establish our social order. We have changed the standards and guidelines that the majority of the American people have lived by for years. Never has a society changed its standards of living in such a short period of time as we Americans have over the past thirty-to-forty years.

"If you can get away with it, then it is all right" has become the new moral code for many Americans. Moral actions, which were "unthinkable" thirty-to-forty years ago, have become "commonplace." Personal accountability, respect for authority and self-control have become an antiquated way of thinking. Nothing, it seems, is indecent or repugnant. Rules and boundaries are resisted and fought against. Very little deserves to be honored and respected. We are told that everyone should be tolerant of the 'new' moral standards.

The report card on our society's new moral standards in a recent thirty year period reads: Crime increased by 500%; illegitimate births increased by 400%; three times the number of children were living in single-parent homes; the teenage suicide rate tripled; the divorce rate doubled; over 40 million babies were murdered through abortion; it became okay to openly teach homosexuality as an acceptable lifestyle in our public schools; the entertainment industry can display sexual permissiveness and violence with very little resistance; child molestation and incest became a national disaster and the police state only 25% of the cases are reported; our children began to gun down their peers and teachers at school; respect for authority declined dramatically; every day the newspapers began to be crowded with reports of robbery, murder, hate, greed, violence and other horrors.

Most Christians, including many Christian leaders, are bewildered by the rapid moral deterioration that has taken place in our country in this last generation. They admit, whatever the root cause, the problem is not being conquered with any degree of success.

There is an important biblical truth we need to remember that is taught throughout the Bible. Ever since God created Adam and Eve, God and His people have always had a spiritual enemy. The Bible calls him Satan or the Devil.

At the very beginning of God's creation and continuing throughout the spiritual history of mankind, Satan has always developed a plan to sabotage any spiritual work of God in an attempt to destroy God's purpose.

There are literally hundreds of examples from history that illustrate Satan's maneuvers in his attempt to destroy God's plan for mankind. I will list just a few, some of which I am sure will be familiar to you.

Of course, Satan's first act was to persuade Eve and then Adam to disobey God. Did you know that Adam and Eve only had one command to obey? That's right, only one command! It is found in Genesis 2:17. This verse says, **"But you must not eat from the tree of the knowledge of good and evil..."**

You wouldn't think that would be difficult, would you? The keeping of just one command! Yet, Satan, in his crafty way was able to deceive first Eve and then Adam and cause them to disobey God's one command. He used the technique of **deception**, which the Bible says will be his main technique of attack in our day.

Another example is the way Satan caused lawlessness and wickedness to become so terrible during Noah's time, that God had no choice but to cleanse the Earth by a flood.

As you travel throughout the Old Testament, you find Satan would often develop a spirit of rebellion and permissiveness in the race God chose to represent Him on Earth, the nation of Israel. At times it would become so strong that these people would completely rebel against the ways of God. This was their condition when God came to Earth Himself in the person of Jesus Christ. They not only didn't recognize Him, they crucified Him.

In the first 300 years of church history, Satan's attacks against Christians, working primarily through the Roman government, were so harsh that an estimated three million Christians were persecuted for their faith by every cruel act of torture imaginable. They were hunted down and thrown to wild animals, torn to pieces, beheaded, burned, crucified and buried alive.

Satan's attacks on the church continued during the historic periods known as the Dark and Middle Ages. The attacks were so severe during this period of time the church operated mostly in secret through the underground.

After Martin Luther posted his "95 theses" on the church door in Wittenberg, Germany on October 31, 1517, the Reformation began and the gospel of Jesus Christ began to openly be preached. Satan, however, continued his attacks against Christians during the Reformation wars when thousands of Christians were brutally massacred in country after country. This was less than 500 years ago!

No doubt you have heard about some of these historical events. There was "St. Bartholomew's Massacre." That occurred in France on August 24, 1572. On that day 70,000 Christians were massacred.

In Spain the effects of the famous "Spanish Inquisition" left over 100,000 people dead and a reported 1,500,000 were banished from the country. Some historians believe Spain has never fully recovered.

In the 32 year period between 1566 and 1598, over 100,000 Christians were slaughtered in the Netherlands.

By the year 1600, approximately 80% of the four million people that populated the country of Bohemia were Christians. Historians report nearly all of the 3,200,000 Christians in that country were exterminated by a crusade during the Reformation wars.

There are many, many more accounts of Satan and his attacks against God's people. He is a wicked and ruthless adversary. To use a phrase coined in our country, "he always plays hardball."

By the year 1700, the major thrust of biblical Christianity had moved across the sea from Europe to the land called America—a land it seems the Lord had kept from being explored until after the Reformation.

Until this last generation the standards that the majority of Americans have lived by have been based on biblical teachings. Therefore, because of our Christian heritage, it is logical to conclude that some day Satan is going to launch an all-out attack against our homeland. There is nothing in Scripture or history that would indicate anything different. All of my research tells me that at some point in time Satan is going to do everything he can to change every law or standard in our country that is based on Christian standards. The body of Christ in America should expect that.

I have prepared and written the message in this book to help you understand how, in this generation, Satan has launched a major spiritual war against our country's Christian heritage.

He is battling for the hearts and minds of the American people. I share the strategy the Bible says Satan is using in this warfare.

I believe the results of this warfare show most Christians in America are not spiritually prepared to stand against the **deceptive** spiritual battles currently taking place in our society. Why do I say that? Look at the hundreds of thousands of Christians who have been hurt in the process of this warfare. Christian families have been devastated and many individual Christian lives are afflicted with hurt and pain. Christian leaders are falling into sin, as well as church members, Christian friends and relatives. The most alarming thing is the fact that it is happening at an accelerated pace all over the country.

The divorce rate among Christians is now reported to be higher than the divorce rate among non-Christians. Immorality, dishonesty, and greed are running rampant in the body of Christ. Bill McCartney, founder of Promise Keepers, told me addiction to pornography has become a national epidemic among Christian men.

Dr. Billy Graham stated a few years ago that, according to his research, at least 90 percent of all Christians in America are living defeated spiritual lives. Others who are in a position to know the spiritual pulse of America have made similar statements. Most pastors and Christian counselors agree with Dr. Graham. These pastors and counselors report that the demands on their time by Christians is overwhelming as they try to handle the problems Christians are having.

Christians readily admit they do not understand the root cause of the rapid breakdown in the moral fiber that has taken place in our society. The majority have not realized that we are living in one of the toughest times ever to be a committed Christian. Why is this a true statement? Because never in the history of mankind has the world had so much power to teach so many people its standards as American society can now teach people through TV, radio, movies, the Internet, dozens of publications, and the secular educational system.

No longer do you and I have to go out into the world in order to make contact with it. Its influencing power seems to come and search us out.

The Christian family has never felt the power and pull of a worldly society such as the one we must contend with today in America. We are being hit daily in every way imaginable to bend and compromise biblical standards. We are living in the middle of a spiritual war zone and many Christians have become casualties as they have suffered major spiritual defeats in their lives.

You may not like to talk about the subject of spiritual warfare, especially if the circumstances surrounding your own personal life appear to be going just fine. Warfare can be exhaustive. It is usually stressful. It may even be expensive and dangerous at times.

However, as a Christian living in America today, you really do not have a choice. There is a spiritual battle taking place to destroy the biblical standards that the majority of Americans once honored and lived by. Not one of us, regardless of how hard we may try, can avoid the spiritual conflicts coming from the influence of this warfare. It is impossible! The worldly standards that we are being taught coming from our world communication system are just too strong.

At the National Prayer Breakfast held February 5, 1998, Billy Graham was interviewed by *USA TODAY* newspaper. Reflecting on our society and on himself, two of the things he said were, *"There was a time when our conscience was more tender. It has become hardened and deadened. That's a danger. We don't detect sin as we used to. We need to search our own hearts."* When speaking of his own accomplishments he said, *"I have in many ways failed...I haven't lived a life of devotion, meditation and prayer. I've allowed the world to creep into my life way too much."*

I think all of us would agree that we have allowed the world to creep into our life way too much. This has caused us to lower many of the biblical standards that have been the fabric and the unwritten guidelines the majority of American people have lived by throughout our history until recent years.

Josh McDowell, one of our country's best known Christian authors and speakers, launched an intensive teaching campaign against this problem in our society. He states that there is a Cultural Revolution taking place in America that is affecting more lives than the Industrial Revolution.

His campaign is called "Right from Wrong." He and several Christian youth leaders from around the nation who are working with him have done a tremendous amount of research on the subject of how the standards of living are rapidly changing among the youth in our country. They conducted several public polls and many interviews. Using the statistical data they accumulated from their research, they concluded that in America: *"Truth has become a matter of taste; morality has been replaced by individual preference; our culture no longer teaches an objective standard of right and wrong; and our society now teaches us that we should be tolerant of another person's beliefs on any of these issues."*

I have prepared a simple graph that illustrates how the biblical standards people lived by in our society have systematically been lowered or removed in the last few years.

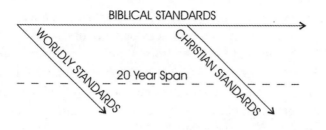

As illustrated by the top line on this graph, biblical standards always remain the same. The line on the left illustrates how over the last fifty years or so the worldly standards in our society have been deteriorating. The line on the right illustrates how over the same period of time many Christian standards have also deteriorated.

This deterioration of Christian standards has come about because during this last generation, many of us began to establish our Christian standards by comparing them to the world's standards rather than by using only biblical truths to make our comparison.

We have maintained the same distance between world standards and Christian standards. We are not as bad as the world, so to speak. But it has been a deceptive trick of the enemy to get us to compare Christian standards with the world rather than with biblical teachings. This has caused us to lower many of the Christian standards in our society. The net result is that what was considered a world standard in American society 20 to 30 years ago has now become an acceptable Christian standard.

This trick of Satan has caused you and me to become more tolerant and indifferent to many of the sins described in the Bible. It has brought devastation to the lives of many Christians because sooner or later, sin leads to broken lives. The Bible puts it very bluntly; **"the wages of sin is death..."** (Romans 6:23).

This does not only apply to salvation. Sin is usually the cause for broken relationships and the inner hurt and pain we suffer.

Satan is using the same strategy on Christians today that he used on Adam and Eve. The story of his attack against Adam and Eve is told in Genesis 3:1-6. You may recall he first placed doubt in Eve's mind about the one command God had given them to obey, which was not to eat the fruit from a certain tree in the garden. But rather than rejecting this doubt and standing firm on God's Word, Eve began to reason in her own mind the right and wrong of this situation. Satan tempted her to question the truth of what God had told her and Adam.

The Bible says the fruit was very attractive to the eye and that it was good for food. In his temptation, Satan threw in another persuasive appeal by telling Eve this fruit would also give her wisdom. This caused her to consider these possibilities because the fruit did offer many benefits for her enjoyment and needs. Because of **deception** she did not deal with the fact that the enemy's temptation would cause her to disregard the truth of God's Word.

This opened the door for Satan to follow up his first temptation and place an outright denial in Eve's mind concerning God's Word. Satan convinced Eve to believe that God did not really mean what He had told her and Adam—that to eat the fruit would be disobedient and would bring death. Genesis 3:13 reads, **"Then the Lord God said to the woman, 'What is this you have done?' The woman said, 'The serpent deceived me, and I ate.'"** Satan convinced her to reason and decide right from wrong for herself rather than trusting and being obedient to the truth of God's Word.

Working through the power of our society to influence us via the communication media and various other means that are available to him, Satan is breaking down our resistance to those standards of the world that are contrary to the biblical truths found in God's Word.

His ability to do this seems overwhelming at times. If we begin to reason in our mind and become tolerant of some of the world's standards or even accept some of its standards— Boom! We have opened the door for Satan to move in. He will bring about defeat to the unsuspecting in this day of tremendous temptation.

The fruits produced in our society this last generation are pointing to the fact that we Americans have fallen into a **spiritual trap of deception** like the frog that was put into a pan of cold water. The water is then slowly heated so that the frog does not notice the water becoming warm. As the water continues to heat to a boil the frog is gradually overcome and never legitimately tries to escape. He didn't become alarmed because the change was not sudden. Therefore, he paid very little attention to what was happening and became a casualty to his environment. He was overcome because he had fallen into **deception**. It cost him his life! This is happening in America and it seems there are only a few people concerned.

The disease of spiritual deception has caused Christians to become indifferent, and therefore, complacent about the rapid deterioration of our country's moral standards. It is why *the world's influence on Christians in this generation has been much greater than the influence of God's standards that are taught in His Word.* What was permissible by worldly standards in America ten, twenty, or thirty years ago is now largely acceptable to Christians. We are more tolerant and apathetic to many of the sins described in the Bible that have become commonplace in our culture.

For the moral character of the people in the world to change is understandable. History reveals the majority of non-Christians will usually follow trends of a society, but for Christians it is different. We are a new creation, born again to be the righteousness of God and live by His biblical code of morals.

Like Eve, and then Adam, Satan's main method of attack in our country has been through **spiritual deception** rather that **persecution**. This scheme of attack has been very successful in America. In addition to tearing down the moral standards in our nation, he has successfully destroyed many of our families, including a lot of Christian families.

I am no different than most people. I would rather dwell on the positives instead of the negatives. However, when you see that you are continually losing the ballgame, you cannot continue to hide you head in the sand. The only way the positives will become more common than the negatives is to address the negative issues and correct them. In the chapters that follow I will examine those Scriptures that will help **you *Prepare Yourself* for our troubled times** that we have been experiencing in our society.

A PROPHETIC WARNING FROM JESUS

1

In the days of Noah, God warned of a coming catastrophe. Noah tried to warn the people of his day, but his words fell on deaf ears. God warned Lot before He rained down fire and sulfur from Heaven and destroyed the people of Sodom. God has also warned the people in our day. His warnings have come mainly through His Word, the Bible, as well as several Christian leaders in our country who have said they have a major concern that America is racing toward God's judgment—Dr. Billy Graham, David Wilkerson, Dr. Henry Blackaby, James Robison, Pat Robertson, Tommy Barnett, Larry Burkett, Bill McCartney—to name a few.

Sexual sins, the dissolution of families, greed, dishonesty, and the deterioration of other moral standards are some of the fruits in our society and in the church that have brought about a major concern that we may fall under God's hand of discipline or judgment. These fruits are the result of **spiritual deception**. However, one of God's most significant Bible warnings concerning **spiritual deception** in our day came from Jesus. It deals with a different type of deception. It has become a major spiritual problem, one which has seriously afflicted the

23

American people. Jesus warned: **"Just as it was in the days of Noah, so also will it be in the days of the Son of Man. People were eating, drinking, marrying and being given in marriage up to the day Noah entered the ark. Then the flood came and destroyed them all. It was the same in the days of Lot. People were eating and drinking, buying and selling, planting and building. But the day Lot left Sodom, fire and sulfur rained down from heaven and destroyed them all. It will be just like this on the day the Son of Man is revealed"** (Luke 17:26-30).

God places a tremendous amount of importance on this prophetic warning from Jesus that addresses the people living near the time of Jesus' return. **Which would be us!** We know these verses are important because the Bible says most of what Jesus said and did was not recorded—I repeat—not recorded in Scripture. **"Jesus did many other things as well. If every one of them were written down, I suppose that even the whole world would not have room for the books that would be written"** (John 21:25). The Bible makes a point that if everything Jesus said and did was recorded, it would be so much it caused John to suppose the whole world would not have room for the books that would be written.

Since John tells us that most of what Jesus said and did was not recorded in the Bible this would mean that anything God did choose to put in the Bible, that Jesus said about our day, is extremely important and therefore we need to take it to heart. That makes these verses from Luke comparing the days of Noah and Lot to our day extremely critical for the body of Christ today.

Jesus said very little about the times in which we now live. Or if He did, God chose not to record it in Scripture. Of all the things that Jesus could have said about the times in which we live, the one God had recorded and has passed on to warn us about our day are these verses in Luke 17:26-30, quoted earlier at the beginning of this chapter.

You may want to reread these verses from Luke 17:26-30 about the days of Noah and Lot! Did you notice that there is something missing in this passage of Scripture? Jesus doesn't mention the many evil gross sins that were taking place in Noah's day or Lot's day. Nor does He say anything about the many gross sins now taking place in our day. In fact, not one of the things He warns us about are a sin. They are the everyday normal things people do in living this life: drinking, eating, marrying, buying, selling, planting and building. It is important to recognize this fact to properly understand the full meaning of this prophecy.

The Old Testament Scriptures state that in the days of Noah and Lot lawlessness, permissiveness and rebellion were running rampant. This was the reason God had to destroy both of those societies. Yet, when comparing our day to those days of Noah and Lot, Jesus does not make one comment about this fact. His comparison is with the buying, selling, eating, drinking, marrying, planting, and building. The everyday normal affairs of life! WHY?

If Jesus knew all about the terrible sins taking place in Noah's day and the crime, violence, sexual permissiveness, abortion, child abuse and other sins that would be going on in our world today, why does He only warn us about the normal things of everyday life? What is He trying to tell us? What is the purpose of His warning?

The answer to that question takes us to the very core of the spiritual warfare now taking place in our country. It helps explain why the moral values of our society have deteriorated so quickly.

Another point that we need to remember in our discussion about these verses from Luke is when God warns His people, it often deals with an area that is not obvious to human wisdom. It covers a subject which requires the Lord's insight. His warnings are directed to areas that are taking us out from under His hedge of protection—areas that will hurt or possibly destroy us spiritually.

These verses I have quoted from Luke comparing our day to Noah's is a warning that carries a much deeper and far greater concern to the Lord than the many gross sins that are now taking place in our society. Everyone knows about the many gross sins. That is why Jesus did not have to mention them. We don't have to be warned about that. We hear about it and read about it every day. David Wilkerson, Pastor of Times Square Church in New York City and one of our country's spiritual leaders stated, *"I was listening to a special radio program in a large eastern city, where the people on the street were being interviewed about the moral condition of America. The question was asked, 'Do you believe America has lost its moral integrity?' Almost all who were interviewed said basically the same thing. 'America is going to hell in a hand basket!' 'We no longer care if scoundrels run our country, as long as we prosper.' 'Anything goes now; we are in the last days of our society—we are modern Rome going into collapse!' 'Morality and purity have been sold out to pleasure and prosperity.' 'Sodom had no porno, no Internet sex, no abortion, no filthy television polluting that society, so how can America expect to go on without being held accountable?'"*

In this warning from God that compares our day to the days of Noah and Lot I see God pouring out His love to the majority of the people—people like you and me—the average person on the street, rather than the minority who are involved in gross sins. We are the Lord's main concern in this warning. All who go about doing those things that people do in the normal way of living their life—the buying, selling, building, marrying, and so forth.

Why are we, the average citizens, Jesus' main concern in His warning about our times, rather than those people who are involved in the many gross sins taking place? Looking ahead God gave us this prophetic warning about the last days because He could see that one of the greatest concerns about the people living in our day would be their over-commitment to these everyday affairs of life—buying, selling building, etc. What we are doing is not a sin. Our sin is the commitment of our heart to these self-serving affairs of everyday life over and above our commitment to live by the standards of God. That is what happened in the days of Noah and it is happening today! Our everyday affairs have become more important to us than our seeking to understand and obey God's standards.

This is exactly what has happened to us in America! The influence of the worldly ways of our society in which we live has become so strong, it has changed the attitude of the majority of the people towards their everyday affairs.

You and I are the people who could help put a stop to our society's morality falling apart at the seams. We are the people who could make a difference. But rather than doing anything about it, Jesus saw that the majority of the people in our day became so wrapped up in their own everyday lives—their own little world so to speak—the buying, selling, building, planting, marrying—that they ignored all of the warning signs.

The signs are everywhere that our nation is on the brink of a great chastening from the hand of God. Why do I say that? Because our nation has been blessed by God far above most nations throughout history. The Bible says that God will hold us accountable for the deterioration of our society's moral standards. Luke 12:48b reads: **"From everyone who has been given much, much will be demanded; and from the one who has been entrusted with much, much more will be asked."** The Scriptures teach God disciplines or brings judgment on those He has blessed if they become misguided and careless in their style of living. It is His way of correcting those He loves (see Hebrews 12:6).

Jesus saw that our lives were being dominated by the everyday affairs of life just like the people in the days of Noah. In these days of great prosperity, we are so busy with our everyday affairs most people don't even believe that judgment is possible. No wonder this was the Lord's main concern! Like it was in the days of Noah, people are doing very little to prepare themselves, which is the only way we are going to keep God's hand of judgment from falling.

What Jesus has warned us about are the symptoms of a spiritual warfare that has developed into a very self-centered, self-serving people—including Christians. This condition caused the Lord more concern than the many gross sins the minority of the people were involved in. He was more concerned with the heart attitude He saw in the majority. The focus of the heart was a problem in Noah's day and He warns it will be a problem in our day. That is why He lists the things that have to do with our everyday affairs even though not one of them is a sin.

The everyday affairs of life caused the downfall of the people in the days of Noah and Lot, and Jesus has warned us that the same thing will cause our downfall. We have become so preoccupied with these everyday affairs of life that serve ourselves—the buying, selling, building, eating, planting, and marrying—that our hearts have grown cold towards a dedicated commitment to live by biblical standards. The worldly media has deceived us and caused us to lose our ability to know right from wrong concerning our commitment to these everyday things.

Also, as Jesus said it would be like it was in the days of Noah, these things have caused us to lose our discernment in interpreting the signs of the times. This too has become a major deceptive snare in our society because of the overpowering ability our society has to influence our commitment to these everyday affairs of life. Jesus warned that even the elect (Christians) would be **deceived** in our day (see Matthew 24:24 and Mark 13:22).

One question that you may ask is: Why does Jesus include the institution of marriage in His warning about these everyday affairs of life? Marriage is actually an excellent example of the things He warns us about because we can clearly see how far off track we have gotten through the institution of marriage, much more than we might through some of the other items He lists. Look at the way He mentions marriage: **"...marrying and being given in marriage..."** This speaks to the way people in our society have lost their commitment to the marriage vows and feel so free to marry again and again—even though God says, **"I hate divorce"** (Malachi 2:16). Divorce and remarrying has become a plague in our society resulting in what sociologists call "serial monogamy."

The basic institution of marriage is certainly not wrong. In fact, it is highly honored by the Lord. It was at a wedding where Jesus performed His first miracle. But the attitude that many have developed in our day about the sanctity of marriage is a good reflection of how far off we have also gotten in handling the other affairs of everyday life that Jesus mentions.

Prepare Yourself

The moral standards of permissiveness and lawlessness deteriorated to the point of being completely out of control in the days of Noah and Lot. But Jesus says there was a greater concern. It was the heart attitude of the people to serve themselves above what is normal. An attitude that caused people not to believe—pay any attention to—the warnings of a coming judgment from the hand of God. Therefore, the people made little or no physical or spiritual preparation. What they were doing was not sinful but the commitment of their heart to these self-serving things drew them away from their commitment to walk according to God's standards and prevented them from seeing the signs of the times. They became blinded by them.

Jesus saw this same condition becoming a very serious problem in our day. By His comments, what He is saying is that the majority of the people need to be warned about how we have gotten caught up in the ways of the world, not just the gross sins of lawlessness, permissiveness, and rebellion that are taking place.

The truth of this prophecy is a tough issue to discuss because I do not want to discount the blessings of God. But the "spirit of merchandizing" has captured the heart of most Americans, creating an over-commitment to our everyday affairs. Highly skilled advertising that constantly focuses our attention on the ways of the world and a media system to deliver this advertising into our homes combined with easy credit, beautiful shopping malls, and no down payment are some of the things that have contributed to making this prophecy come true.

God chose to put these words of warning from Jesus in the Bible to warn us about our day, and the truth of this prophecy is being fulfilled in America now. God is faithful. It was important to Him that we know the kind of spiritual warfare the enemy would throw at Christians in these end-times. These words of

Jesus describe the essence of what the enemy is using to keep you and me from standing up for and living by God's moral standards. His attacks are very deceptive and very difficult to discern in today's world. That is why so many Christians have fallen into **deception** and become victims of his attacks. Another danger coming from the influence of the worldliness around us is it has caused Christians to lose their discernment about the signs of the times.

SIGN OF THE TIMES: ECONOMICS

Due to the extensive buying, selling, building, planting, Jesus warned us about, a consequence has developed in our society which has caused a major economic problem. To understand this economic problem and how it developed, I must go back to the 1940s right after World War II.

World War II left the nations of Europe and the Pacific Rim in shambles. Many people not only lost their homes, they lost their means of livelihood as well.

The fighting destroyed factories, businesses, power plants, roads, bridges, rail lines and much more. Germany, England, Japan, and many other nations lost their industrial capacity. The infrastructure needed for economic productivity had been wiped out by the war.

These nations also lost a whole generation of industrial and government managers during the war—the leadership necessary for business enterprise. Consequently, the economic strength of these nations experienced a severe setback. England, for example, has never really recovered. After the war it went from being an industrial power with globe-encircling interests to a declining nation with a modest role in today's international affairs.

While the European and Pacific powers crawled out from under the rubble of World War II, the United States was on its way to economic supremacy. World War II actually enhanced America's economic position.

None of the fighting had occurred on American soil, so we emerged as the only major world power with its industrial and agricultural output intact. This allowed the development of a lifestyle for the people in our country that was unheard of before the war.

Production within American factories after the war continued at a steady clip, as we were in a very unique position to furnish our wartime allies and enemies with many of the products and services the people in these countries needed. This allowed the average United States worker to have a steady job with a good income. Few of those in the industrial world could boast higher pay, more extensive fringe benefits, or better working conditions.

During the next 30 years after World War II, American products achieved worldwide reputation. We were the emerging "great society."

The postwar years gave American companies a tremendous head start. The lack of foreign competition, combined with Yankee know-how, put us into a unique leadership position in many areas that did not exist before the war. The United States captured first place in the production of automobiles, machine tools, electronic equipment, and many other vital industries. American factories became models of industrial excellence as American technology and management expertise set the standard.

Not surprisingly, few Americans wanted to buy foreign imports, which were badmouthed as shoddy imitations. We preferred our high quality domestic products to the second rate goods being manufactured abroad. This, along with the fact that we were providing the major share of the goods and services needed around the world, created an impressive trade surplus. For many years following the war, Americans sold far more in foreign countries than they bought, and billions of excess dollars from around the world poured into the US economy.

As a result, the American standard of living shot up beyond imagination. The average American family claimed vast worldly possessions that were unprecedented in the history of mankind. With less than 7% of the world's population, we accumulated half of the world's wealth and consumed a full third of the world's resources each year. This availability of consumer goods allowed Americans to have a higher standard of living than virtually every other nation throughout the world. That was not the case before World War II.

During the post war years, those categorized as "poor" in America would have been considered "upper class" in many other countries. The American lifestyle became the envy of the world as Americans routinely enjoyed products and services completely out of reach for people in other lands. I am not saying there was anything wrong with this, I am just reporting on our economic history as it relates to the development of the lifestyle Jesus warns us about.

However, by the mid 70s, the tide of our economic supremacy began to turn. The military obligations the United States had incurred around the globe following the war meant massive government spending. The American economy became dependent on foreign oil, and the oil producing nations organized to charge more.

American industries began to lose their technological edge. More important, the rest of the world was regaining its industrial capacity. European and Asian competitors caught up with and even began to pass us within industries pioneered in the United States.

Imported clothing, Asian electronic goods, and foreign cars meant value for the American consumer. And, for the first time in half a century, Americans began buying more products overseas than they were selling. Rather than a healthy trade surplus, we began to generate a massive trade deficit.

We began to put ourselves in a difficult financial situation. We should have scaled down our standard of living to meet our diminished economic position in the world, but it would have been a political disaster for our government leaders to tell the American people of this economic truth.

Therefore, the expectations of most Americans *increased,* not *decreased.* We had more than most people anywhere in the world and enjoyed a standard of living unknown in the history of mankind. But we had been led to expect this lifestyle as our birthright, and it was getting harder and harder to achieve. This began to create a tremendous debt problem.

We no longer had the billions of dollars that exports pumped into our economy when we were supplying the rest of the world with the majority of its needed goods and services. And, with the many new goods and services our society had to offer, most Americans had to find a new way to finance their desired standard of living, which was to borrow.

For most Americans, the over commitment to buying, selling, building, planting, that Jesus warned about became a matter of ignoring economic reality. The widening gap between what we expected and what most Americans were capable of paying for, led us to a dependence on credit. Consequently, we have fallen into heavy debt. Personal debt has reached record highs and is still accelerating. Government debt is in the same boat. Credit abuse has put a stranglehold on our economy.

Prepare Yourself

What I want you to see is this: by supplying the rest of the world with many of its goods and services in the generation after World War II, Americans were able to enjoy a standard of living unheard of in the history of mankind. But, after the other industrialized countries regained their ability to supply their people with many of their goods and services, this took a big chunk out of the demand for our products; therefore, dollars were taken out of our economy.

This brought about an economic condition in which the only way the majority of Americans could continue to maintain their high standard of living was through credit. The last several years of our prosperous time has been financed on credit cards. The insurmountable debt that has resulted casts a gloomy shadow over America's economic future. Most people do not have enough cash in their savings account to get them through even a short period of difficult economic times.

At the root of our economic vulnerability is our failure to live within our means. Installment debt, mortgage debt, government debt, business debt, foreign debt and other private debt has risen in a vain effort to maintain our present standard of living. **We have mortgaged the future to pay for the present.** To illustrate just how bad this debt problem has become I will review **Consumer Debt**. This is an indebtedness that is close to home.

Outstanding consumer debt—not counting real estate—in our country was $296 billion dollars in 1982. It has now passed 1.5 trillion. That is five times higher than what it was just a few years ago. As mentioned that does not include real estate debt. The average total consumer installment debt, such as credit cards, now outstrips total income. On average, American families owe $8,367 in credit card debt alone. They pay an average of 14% of their income to credit card debt and 50% have difficulty making the minimum monthly payments. Excessive debt is the major deterrent to biblical giving, and financial stress is the #1 reported cause of divorce. [Source: The Association of Church Financial Ministries.]

The "spirit of merchandizing" has truly captured the heart of most Americans, creating an over-commitment to our everyday affairs just as Jesus prophesied in Luke 17:26-30. Many Christians in America now seek **first** for their own well-being rather than to seek first the Lord and how they may serve Him. The Bible states: **"But seek first his kingdom and his righteousness, and all these things will be given to you as well. Therefore do not worry about tomorrow, for tomorrow will worry about itself. Each day has enough trouble of its own"** (Matthew 6:33,34).

For many American families, two incomes are now necessary to meet debt obligations. The loss of one income, even for a brief period, could put them dangerously close to financial ruin. Overall personal bankruptcies have climbed from 300,000 per year in 1980 to 1.4 million per year in 1997. What is so alarming about this is that we are living in a time of prosperity! Imagine what will happen if the economy weakens.

Needless to say, millions of Americans will be in serious financial trouble if we experience a decline in the economy.

Many economists believe the problem of our debt-ridden US economy has reached the point of no return and appears to be irreversible.

Do you remember the stock market crash of October 19, 1987? It is easy for my wife, Barbara, and me to remember that day because we were in Zurich, Switzerland. I was there attending a worldwide economic seminar for the metals industry. Several top economists from around the world were present at this meeting.

Prepare Yourself

That crash in 1987 came and has gone without serious fall-out. However, at the time many people expressed great concern because the crash sent a clear message that our country's financial and economic condition was not very stable. Economists have said that no matter what triggered that Black Monday, if our financial markets were sound, a plunge of this speed and magnitude could not have happened.

They point out this is just one of several indicators over the past several years that warn us of a substantial weakness within our economic structure.

The failure of the savings-and-loans a few years ago was another warning. The cost of that bailout was around $500 billion dollars to the American people. These and other events are warnings of an underlying structural problem in our economy.

During the 1980s, our country shifted from being the largest creditor nation in the world to becoming the largest debtor nation. That was a huge turn in our economic status!

We have now dug ourselves into a financial hole of debt so deep we will never be able to climb out. It appears to make no difference whether the government taxes more or taxes less; the debt will continue to grow.

In a larger sense, what the government does or doesn't do at this point will not make a lot of difference. The years of our overspending cannot be paid back. Current "solutions" to the debt crisis amount to economic fiction rather than sound economic thinking. No conventional solutions are available because this is an unheard-of economic problem. No matter what the politicians promise, record indebtedness will ultimately result in financial judgment.

Sooner or later, the American people will be forced to accept a dramatically different standard of living. It's hard to say what will ultimately be the straw that breaks the camel's back—which shock to the economy will trigger a major economic collapse. But many economists say it is inevitable. When it does take place it will probably shake the world. The whole world is dependent on our economy. Isaiah prophesied, **"The arrogance of man will be brought low and the pride of men humbled; the Lord alone will be exalted in that day, and the idols will totally disappear. Men will flee to caves in the rocks and to holes in the ground from dread of the Lord and the splendor of his majesty, when he rises to shake the earth...Stop trusting in man, who has but a breath in his nostrils. Of what account is he?"** (Isaiah 2:17-19, 22).

When will this happen? I certainly don't know. It could be this year, next year, ten or twenty years from now. I do know that as Jesus warns, **"...as it was in the days of Noah,"** very few people are making proper preparations. They are too caught up in the affairs of this life to consider such things.

What will happen when the standard of living we have known for so long begins to evaporate? No one can precisely predict. There could be significant social and political fallout associated with any major economic catastrophe. A major financial panic might bring civil disorder, violence, and unimaginable chaos.

Because there is so much lawlessness today, so much crime in our society, the majority of people will probably look to the government to do something if and when such a financial crisis hits our economy. The government will have great incentive to eliminate perceived threats to the economy by extending control over buying and selling. When the next major economic shock provokes deep-seated fear, people will cry out to the government to do whatever it takes to save them.

It is difficult to say what all these commercial regulations might entail, but Bible prophecy clearly points to the day when a beast-superpower will control economic transactions. A marking system of some kind will be imposed. John, the writer of the book of Revelation, states, **"He** [referring to the beast-superpower] **also forced everyone, small and great, rich and poor, free and slave, to receive a mark on his right hand or on his forehead, so that no one could buy or sell unless he had the mark, which is the name of the beast or the number of his name. This calls for wisdom. If anyone has insight, let him calculate the number of the beast, for it is man's number. His number is 666"** (Revelation 13:16-18). He ties the marking system to the beast's control of the economy. Exactly what form this economic control will take cannot be answered with absolute certainty. However, a marking system like the kind John describes has already been developed.

In fact, such a marking system has been in operation since 1973. It is called the Universal Product Code. This code identifies practically every item found in grocery and retail stores.

The August 25, 1974, issue of the Los Angeles Times explains it by saying, *"The grocery store industry has developed what it calls the Universal Product Code (UPC), which to the consumer looks like a series of vertical lines covering an area about the size of a large postage stamp."*

What is of interest from the perspective of Bible prophecy is that every UPC code contains three unidentified marks corresponding to the number 666. Students of Bible prophecy know that sixes are among the secrets of the economy destined to close out this, the Gentile Age.

These three sixes are the key working numbers for every version of the UPC code. Computer experts I consulted told me that the triple-six pattern has become a universal design standard; it cannot be changed.

Most of the marks, or bars, in the UPC symbol are identified by numbers at the bottom of each mark. But there are always at least three bars that are not identified. Look at some of the bar codes found on products in your home. If you had the standard for interpreting these bar codes, you would discover three of these unidentified marks are always the number 6. This is true for every bar code you want to look at. Three unidentified marks on any UPC code you inspect always translate into three sixes. The number 666! That cannot be changed!

FIGURE ONE

0 7 7 9 7 5 0   2 2 6 5 8 8

MOST COMMON UPC CODE

All of the marks, or bars, in figure one are identified by numbers at the bottom of the code except for three marks. The mark at the far right, in the middle and at the far left are not identified.

FIGURE TWO

1   2   3

6   6   6

In figure two I have isolated the three marks that are not identified in figure one. There are always at least three unidentified marks in every UPC code. Three of these unidentified marks are always the number "6" uncovering the coded use of the number "666" in every bar code.

Why is the number six used? Computer technicians say that 6 is the perfect computer number. Six is the perfect number

41

because computers work on a series of six cores that allow current to change direction in order to perform switching operations.

The formula for this system is 6 60 6. To number a card, person, or item, the transaction must be prefixed six hundred, threescore, and six, just as John said in Revelation 13:18. **Only through the inspiration of the Holy Spirit could John have written about marks that are associated with the three numbers of 666.** An interesting side note is the number 6 in Scripture is always related to man and his activities. It is man's number as John says in this prophecy recorded in Revelation 13:18.

Although the bar codes (the marks) on grocery items are the most noticeable, credit and bank cards (Visa, Mastercard, etc.) make use of the same bar code marks. These are micro-encoded along the magnetic strip on the back of the card. Literally tens of thousands of characters can be micro-encoded on the three by one-half inch magnetic strip on the back of a single card. It is now possible to generate a personal record of every person's purchases, transactions, and so on to control buying and selling.

The technology for a cashless society exists. Credit cards make the introduction of a national identification card possible right now. Existing laser technology could be used to implant information beneath the skin on the head, arm, or some other place on the body.

Capsule implants—computer chips—injected beneath the surface of the skin, are already widely promoted as hidden identification tags for tracking valuable livestock—cats, dogs, cattle, and other animals.

The possibility for a national state-of-the-art, tamper-proof numbering system with an implantation device in the head, arm or somewhere on the body is now available and has been discussed by some government officials for use in health care.

The important thing for Christians to realize and understand is that the age of the **"Mark of the Beast"** is here. The resources and know-how to implement what John prophesied over 1900 years ago are already in place.

SIGN OF THE TIMES: SEDUCING (DECEIVING) SPIRITS

3

In the last days shall come seducing (deceiving) spirits (see I Timothy 4:1) that shall turn many away. Many shall fall through various lust and because of sin abounding.

My wife, Barbara, hung up the phone and began to cry. I asked, *"Who was that? What's the matter?"* She replied, *"I just can't take any more."* She had been talking to a Christian friend who had asked my wife if she could come and see us. She and her husband were having difficulties and thinking of separating—our friend was scared and didn't know what to do.

The heartaches Christians are experiencing due to the breakdown in their personal relationships (husband-wife, parents-children and others) have become devastating. One of our country's leading seminaries conducted a survey. They found among the ministers who are filling the pulpits of our churches, the number admitting they have had sexual relations outside their marriage has escalated beyond what I even want to report. Emotional stress and depression are at record levels among our people. Business ethics have never been worse among Christians. This is just a sampling of the many consequences the body of Christ is suffering due to the increased activity of Satan's seducing or deceiving spirits.

My description of the work of seducing or deceiving spirits would be: *Seducing or deceiving spirits tempt God's people to trade the truth of God's Word and to accept something that is contrary to the Word of God. They try to make something wrong seem innocent. To perform their acts of seduction they attempt to make their enticements irresistible. They try to make the difference between black and white seem like a shade of gray. If we do not know the Word of God and diligently seek righteousness, and hate every evil way, then we will become susceptible to these deceiving spirits, as Scripture warns this is one of the greatest dangers in the last days.*

Seducing spirits work by putting thoughts in our mind. They use every means available to interject these thoughts that are contrary to the teachings of God's Word.

We need to be firmly established in God's Word and not in the personalities of men so that we will not be influenced by seducing spirits that are manifesting themselves in our culture. We are to follow the path of righteousness and diligently inquire of the Lord when we hear of something that we may not have seen in the Word. We are not to hold the popularity of a person in admiration, for it is by this method that Satan is deceiving many of God's people.

These are difficult days for Christians to battle deceiving spirits. Never in the history of man has Satan's world system had the power or means to put so many thoughts in the minds of so many people as through our present day mass communication media. We are continuously being bombarded with messages and images that tempt us to accept the standards of the world.

Prepare Yourself

Satan's most effective use of our modern media is through television, the Internet and the movie theater. Their impact is both audible and visual—capturing our time and our minds daily. Anything with the capability of implanting thoughts or ideas into our minds must be thought of as a teacher and a potential deceiver.

Our modern day media has seduced Christians in America to think like, act like, and live like—therefore, have the same problems as—the people of the world. That is how television has affected the overall spiritual standards in our nation and in the church since it came into existence a generation ago.

Tolerance of and, eventually, indifference to sin is the product of exposure to and seduction by the teaching media of our worldly society. By continually putting worldly thoughts into our mind, seducing spirits have been able to lure us away from our commitment to biblical standards and cause us to accept many standards of our society's new moral code.

In order to walk in spiritual victory over the influence of the seducing spirits now at work in our world, it helps if we can understand a vital spiritual truth found in Scripture. The Bible says that when we accepted Jesus Christ into our hearts as our personal savior, we were given the gift of a power source that is greater than the power of our inner sinful nature. It is the Holy Spirit of God, God Himself. We literally become the temple of the Holy Spirit of God when we are reborn spiritually. **"Don't you know that you yourselves are God's temple and that God's Spirit lives in you?"** (I Corinthians 3:16). This new power source is something we cannot see. We only see the effect it has on people through their personality and character changes and the victories they begin to have over sin. The Holy Spirit of God empowers us to walk righteously, to obey God's Word and live a holy life. He motivates holy activities and attitudes in our personal being.

However, the Bible also teaches that even though we now have the Holy Spirit of God living within us, the power within our nature that causes us to sin did not die or go away (see Romans, Chapter seven). We need to be sensitive to this fact that our sinful nature is still there—a part of our inner make-up. Of course, our daily experiences tell us this is true.

This means that everyone who becomes a Christian, a true believer, becomes a battleground for spiritual warfare in his or her thoughts and actions. It is the Holy Spirit of God—who empowers us to walk righteously—at war against our old sinful nature which is being tempted by Satan and the seducing spirits of this world system. To know that this spiritual warfare is occurring on a daily basis is especially important now. Because to live in a world that has the power and ability to put thoughts into our minds and deceive us as our society can, is heavy-duty spiritual warfare.

If the Holy Spirit is going to control our lives over our sinful nature, we cannot allow our minds to be filled with and influenced by the standards of the world. When we do, it opens the door for Satan to deceive us by seducing the desires of our sinful nature. It is amazing how quickly he can cause us to alter, and try to justify, something other than God's Christian standards.

The Bible teaches that our sinful nature consists of three primary desires. They are **"the lust of the flesh, and the lust of the eyes, and the pride of life"** (I John 2:15 KJV). All of Satan's temptations to deceive us are directed towards at least one and sometimes all three of these desires of our sinful nature. They can take on the form of many things: material items, knowledge, sexual attractions, position—almost anything that serves our "self" life.

47

The enemy will even use the name of God to get us to justify something we want. When Satan tempted Jesus, he tempted Him with these same three primary desires of the sinful nature (see Luke 4:1-13). Observe how often you can identify these three lusts of our sinful nature being tempted in TV and movie productions, books and magazines, advertisements, and most other areas of the world media system.

This type of deceptive spiritual warfare is all around us; we encounter it every day. Many Christians are not aware that they are in the middle of such a spiritual battle and therefore constantly expose themselves to the temptation of Satan's seducing spirits as a part of their daily spiritual diet. This can quench the power of the Spirit of God in their lives. When that happens, the inner self-centered desires of the sinful nature become the dominating power source that controls their thoughts and actions.

Some of the heaviest spiritual warfare we contend with today involves the seducing spirits of independence and a strong, self-centered, self-serving nature. The media and other influencing factors in our society constantly portray these characteristics. The Bible tells us where such characteristics originate.

"Who is wise and understanding among you? Let him show it by his good life, by deeds done in the humility that comes from wisdom. But if you harbor bitter envy and selfish ambition in your hearts, do not boast about it or deny the truth. Such 'wisdom' does not come down from heaven but is earthly, unspiritual, of the devil. For where you have envy and selfish ambition, there you find disorder and every evil practice.

But the wisdom that comes from heaven is first of all pure; then peace loving, considerate, submissive, full of mercy and good fruit, impartial and sincere. Peacemakers

who sow in peace raise a harvest of righteousness" (James 3:13-18).

Much is being said about the many temptations that the enemy is using today to turn God's people from His paths. However, I want to briefly discuss three temptations of great danger to our Christian walk that the enemy is using with tremendous success in our society that we don't hear much about. They are very seductive and difficult for us to detect. The three are **worldly possessions, fear of being reviled, and unbelief.**

The **first** temptation, **the acquisition of material possessions,** is being used by the enemy to seduce our natural desires so we over commit our time and our money to obtain things we shouldn't or can't afford.

We live in a culture that has the ability to produce many material things, more than any time in the history of mankind. We also have the professional means to advertise, promote and sell the products our society can produce. This, along with the communication media to deliver the advertising, has created an atmosphere of emotional mind control that is often irresistible to the consumer.

One of the main problems we face in today's spiritual battlefield is how to avoid being seduced by the many temptations being thrown at us concerning material things. These temptations have changed the course of man's response and commitment to the many material things available. The economic indebtedness I discussed in the last chapter is a prime example. We have been seduced into an economic whirlwind of buying and selling that is unprecedented. Our growing indebtedness is destroying the economic structure of our society. Few people pay attention to the fact that we are being seduced into an economic storm whose effects are going to stagger mankind's imagination. No wonder it concerned Jesus so much that He warned us about the buying and selling in the last days. It is a very deceptive method Satan is using to seduce Christians and cause them to become slaves to the world system through debt.

The spiritual danger in this temptation, if we fall victim to its deception, is it causes us to become spiritually dull and sluggish. We are no longer sensitive to the spiritual warnings around us. We develop a false sense of spiritual pride—that we have all things under control. It can cause us to place a greater emphasis on our physical needs and wants than on our spiritual needs.

Money and possessions can become a spiritual power, an object of worship and a rival to our desire to live by God's standard. That is the danger of this temptation. People who love money resort to all kinds of things to get it; it has a way of enslaving the person seeking it.

Satan is successfully using the material things of our world to seduce us into many of his worldly traps. The attachment to so many things of the world is not normal behavior for Christians. It is no longer just a question of food, drink, clothing, and shelter. We are now encountering the work of demons as they attempt to lure us into the ways of this world system. Many Christians have become so attracted and indebted to material possessions in our society that they have little time or funds left for the work of the Lord. In his Screwtape Letters C. S. Lewis stated, *"Prosperity knits a man to the world. He feels that he is 'finding his place in it' 'while really it is finding its place in him.'"*

I am not speaking out against God's blessings because God does bless His people. However, the Bible teaches us to keep our lives free from the love of money and to be content with what we have—whether it is much or little. Paul said, "...I have learned to be content whatever the circumstances. I know what it is to be in need, and I know what it is to have plenty. I have learned the secret of being content in any and every situation, whether well fed or hungry, whether living in plenty or in want. I can do everything through him who gives me strength" (Philippians 4:11-13). Hebrews 13:5 says **"Keep your lives free from the love of money and be content with what you have, because God has said, 'Never will I leave you; never will I forsake you.'"** Jesus admonished us not to be anxious over material things but to recognize that God's kingdom is more important than money. The Bible teaches we are to grow in our trust of God and He will guide us as to how we are to provide for our needs.

"**Therefore I tell you, do not worry about your life, what you will eat or drink; or about your body, what you will wear. Is not life more important than food, and the body more important than clothes? Look at the birds of the air; they do not sow or reap or store away in barns, and yet your heavenly Father feeds them. Are you not much more valuable than they?...But seek first his kingdom and his righteousness, and all these things will be given to you as well"** (Matthew 6:25-26, 33).

A **second** great temptation the enemy is using in America today is to get us to be overly concerned about what people may think of us. We want to avoid being **reviled.** To revile is to discredit, dishonor, berate, put down, make fun of, ridicule or reject. The enemy has seduced Christians today with a fear of standing up against the sins of the world, worried about being reviled. Therefore, we sit idly by and do little to prevent the biblical standards in our society from deteriorating. We are too concerned with our credibility in the eyes of the world. As it was in the days of Noah, we don't want to openly take a stand against sin. We would rather attend to the personal affairs of our life and not be bothered. I don't know about you, but I would like to be like Noah. Because he took a stand, he was able to save his family from the coming storms of judgment.

In the prelude of this book, I mentioned a few of the many sacrifices Christians have made throughout the life of the church in standing up for the cause of Christ and following His standards. In America today we make very few sacrifices for the standards of Christ.

This is evident by the way the attitude of our society has changed so drastically in the last generation. Never has a single society experienced such a breakdown in its moral standards in so short a period of time. The fact that so many Americans feel free to openly live in sin **says** more than anything else of our weakness as Christians to stand up for and live by biblical standards. No longer do we cause conviction in the hearts of non-Christians.

I believe this may be why a few years ago the world began to shout, "God is dead." In my arrogance, like many other Christians, I scoffed at those who where shouting this statement. Of course the statement is not true, but rather than act proud and scoff I should have tried to find out why the world was making such a proclamation. Maybe it was because they saw that most Christians live no differently than the way most people in the world live. As Christians, we are experiencing the same defeats in our lives that the people of the world are experiencing.

Our society's ability to teach and influence us has seduced us into becoming apathetic toward sin. SEDUCTION AND DECEPTION BREED DOMINATION!

A **third** temptation the enemy is using on Christians today that seems to be going unnoticed is **unbelief.** We have been seduced to believe that God will not carry out His judgment against unrighteousness—that God does not really mean what He has said in His Word. It is the same temptation Satan used against Adam and Eve in the garden. It is what caused them to disobey God's Word. Jesus said it will be the same today as it was in the days of Noah. The people then did not believe God's judgment was coming.

The temptation of unbelief has brought a lot of compromise in the body of Christ. Unbelief and compromise go together.

As I stated earlier several of our country's spiritual leaders have declared that America is racing toward judgment. For example, Pat Robertson, President of the Christian Broadcasting Network, writes: *"...Murder, rape, looting, family breakdown, sexual permissiveness, militant homosexuality, blasphemous films and music, the widespread embrace of Satanism and the occult, unbelievable wasteful and luxurious living by the rich, and open denial of God and Christian values by the western establishment—educators, the philosophers, parts of the church, the media, the film community, and government leaders—have opened our society to the very real possibility of devastating judgment by a Holy God. The question is no longer will God's judgment fall on the earth, but when."*[1]

The subject of judgment, or discipline, is not a popular topic. It is, however, one of the most important truths in the Bible. It is God's way of correcting those He loves. **"...the Lord disciplines those he loves"** (Hebrews 12:6). God disciplines His people when they fall into deception and become misguided and careless.

We usually think of judgment as something negative, but, when administered by a loving judge, discipline produces something good. A loving disciplinarian places the overall well-being of those in need of correction above the inner hurt and pain experienced by the one carrying out the discipline. Uncompromising discipline and sacrificial love go hand in hand.

America has benefited from God's blessing over and above most nations throughout its history. This is especially true from a spiritual perspective. Christianity has been the dominant religious faith in America from the beginning. In the year 1892, in the case of The Church of the Holy Trinity verses The United States, The Supreme Court issued 87 precedents in coming to its decision which states: *"Our laws and institutions must necessarily be based upon and embody the teachings of the Redeemer of mankind. It is impossible that it should be otherwise and in this sense and to this extent our civilization and our institutions are emphatically Christian. This is historically true from the discovery of this continent to the present hour; we find everywhere a clear recognition of the same truth. These and many other matters add a volume of unofficial declarations to the mass of organic utterances that this is a Christian nation."* God's miraculous hand in America's spiritual development cannot be denied.

However, we are held accountable for the resources and opportunities God gave us. **"From everyone who has been given much, much will be demanded; and from the one who has been entrusted with much, much more will be asked"** (Luke 12:48b). Clearly, our relationship with the Lord cannot be a one way street. Seeking to live a righteous life is not optional. We are commanded to be holy because God is holy (see I Peter 1:13-16). We are to be the salt of the Earth (the preservers of good), and a light set on a hill (bringing hope to a dark world).

Sign of the Times: Seducing (Deceiving) Spirits

God allows Satan to test our commitment to His righteousness. Our lack of commitment to His biblical standards cannot be hidden for very long and, to be sure, our sin usually becomes known. In this last generation, Satan and the world system have challenged our spiritual walk as never before. We have opened the door to the enemy, and he has flooded our homes with his worldly ways. The result is a collapse of the whole moral structure of our society. With our strong Christian heritage and knowledge of God's Word, we are without excuse. Instead of doing something about our country's moral decay, we have become part of the problem.

With the power of the media in our society to expose and influence us to accept many of its standards, it is not difficult to see why God warned us about these last days. It has become so hard for Christians to stand up for righteousness. To do so often makes you feel like you are just pounding your head against the wall. It is so much easier to give in, be tolerant, and compromise. We know that to rock the boat will only bring more stress and pressure. So why bother? We just go about doing our own thing, taking care of our own affairs, just as Jesus warned would happen in our day.

Unfortunately, that kind of attitude means we have been seduced and deceived by the enemy. The Lord never promised it was going to be a life of ease. Spiritual warfare is not easy. In fact, we are told by Jesus to count the cost. That is because we have been called to become spiritual warriors—Christian soldiers. In the past it has even brought death to some. There are countries where the persecution of Christians is still very strong.

This may be a bold thing to say, but the ease of Christianity in America will soon be coming to an end. We are rapidly approaching the day when to be a biblical Christian in America will require us to make a choice. We are either going to be a spiritual WARRIOR in the Lord's army today, or we will be considered a POW or AWOL by the Lord.

We may or may not have personally helped create the current problem in our society, but we must come face to face with the type of spiritual warfare that is now taking place everywhere. We can no longer ride the fence or hide our head in the sand. Too many lives are being blown away—too many families are being destroyed—and, you and I as Christians, are the only ones who have the true answer to solve these problems. There is no one else. Governments, politicians, and organizations try to come up with innovative programs to stop the moral holocaust taking place in our society, but they will continue to fail. It is up to the body of Christ. You and me!

The Bible teaches that Satan is a powerful spiritual adversary, but it also teaches that as Christians, we do not have to live in fear of him. The Bible says in I John 4:4, **"...the one who is in you** (referring to the Holy Spirit) **is greater than the one who is in the world** (referring to Satan)."

We need to respect the fact that Satan can cause tremendous spiritual damage if we are not prepared to stand against him. We can see what happened in the downfall of Israel and several of her leaders at various times in the Old Testament. We can also look at our own country and how several Christian leaders have fallen in recent years.

This is why we must **be prepared**. In these troubled times in which we live, you must "Prepare Yourself," be on the alert, and sensitive to the spiritual harm of what is taking place around you in our present worldly environment. Learn what is right and what is wrong from a biblical viewpoint and then be strong enough to stand for what is right. Become hungry and thirsty for a life of righteousness, see Matthew 5:7.

In this cold world of darkness, Christians are the only ray of sunlight with any chance of bringing hope to those who are down and out, and even lost. This will only take place if we are willing to stand in the gap and fight the battle that must be fought in order to stop what is happening in our society.

In the world, whether in business, military operations, sports or other endeavors, people spend a lot of time in order to know and understand their competition and know their competitor's strategies. They devote a lot of energy to laying out great plans and then work hard to carefully prepare themselves to implement those plans for their defense and counterattacks. To be successful, people must follow this principle of preparation.

In Christianity our weapons may be different, but in spiritual warfare the principles of our need to prepare ourselves are no different. As more Christians become involved in the fury of the spiritual battle taking place in our country, you can count on Satan to greatly intensify the level of warfare. The battle is going to get a lot worse! Satan is not going to let up. He is going to fight hard until the very end. You need to **be prepared** so you do not become a victim of the cultural revolution taking place in our society.

There is only one answer that will put a stop to the devastation in so many lives. Christians in America must strengthen their position and resist yielding to the standards of the world. This is going to take a strong commitment and a willingness to engage in some heavy spiritual combat on our part.

Most Americans will quickly rise to defend their rights for freedom or to protect their physical homeland. But in the area of spiritual warfare we have lost a lot of our courage. Mark Twain is quoted as saying, *"It is curious that physical courage should be so common in the world and moral courage so rare."*[2] Christianity in our country requires very little sacrifice. As a result we have grown spirituality soft, complacent, lazy, and apathetic about sin.

We have allowed our country to deteriorate spiritually to the point that God may have only one option. To save us from spiritual self-destruction, He may move to judge our nation and discipline its people. There are too many Christian people in our country whom God loves for Him to allow our nation to continue in the direction chosen by this last generation. The author of Hebrews states; **"If we deliberately keep on sinning after we have received the knowledge of the truth, no sacrifice for sins is left, but only a fearful expectation of judgment..."** (Hebrews 10:26,27).

SIGN OF THE TIMES: LAWLESSNESS

4

The Lord gave the Apostle Paul prophetic words about the lawless spirit that would sweep across the central area of Christianity in the end-times. It is found in II Thessalonians 2:1-4 where Paul states, **"Concerning the coming of our Lord Jesus Christ and our being gathered to him, we ask you, brothers, not to become easily unsettled or alarmed by some prophecy, report or letter supposed to have come from us, saying that the day of the Lord has already come. Don't let anyone deceive you in any way, for that day will not come** (the return of Jesus) **until the rebellion occurs and the man of lawlessness is revealed, the man doomed to destruction. He opposes and exalts himself over everything that is called God or is worshiped, and even sets himself up in God's temple, proclaiming himself to be God."**

The purpose of this chapter is not to convince you that we live in a lawless society. This is revealed every day by listening to the news or reading the newspaper. We live in a society where you don't know from one day to the next what unspeakable crime is going to be reported. And all the crimes being committed are not by hardened thugs; even children are going on killing sprees, gunning down other children and teachers at school. I guess we shouldn't be surprised. Many children have watched thousands of murders on television and have been taught there are no moral absolutes, so they see little harm in killing their classmates.

In this chapter, I will look at God's warning in Scripture that reveals the root cause of this spirit of lawlessness we are experiencing in our country.

Statistics confirm that the American people have become the world's most immoral people even though we live in the world's greatest geographical center of Christian teaching. This is hard to understand. This fact points out more than anything else that Christians are not living by biblical moral standards. Our spiritual weakness and lack of spiritual commitment for righteousness in the body of Christ is revealed in that so many Americans no longer have a *"fear of sinning."* The freedom to openly commit sin is a reflection on the American church. We have become so much a part of the world that we don't cause conviction in the people of the world like Christians did in the past.

Satan is conducting one of the greatest **attacks of deception** on God's people in America ever pulled. In this last generation, Satan and his world system have challenged our spiritual walk of righteousness as never before. To take our stand to live the Christian life in our day demands that we put on the full armor of God. The Bible says, **"Finally, be strong in the Lord and in His mighty power. Put on the full armor of God so that you can take your stand against the devil's schemes...so that when the day of evil comes, you may be able to stand your ground"** (Ephesians 6:10-11,13). The day of evil is here. The enemy is challenging every ounce of spiritual authority we have in these last days.

There is not a single Christian who can avoid being called to fight in the army of God in the spiritual warfare now taking place in our country. The Lord is depending on you and me to show the world whose God has the power—theirs or ours! The only way we are going to keep our society from becoming more and more evil, and from sinking deeper and deeper into sin is to take a stand.

God has given Christians in America a rich Christian heritage along with the freedom to live out our faith. It is obvious that Satan is out to destroy every good thing with which God has blessed us.

One of the key prophetic Scriptures about the end-times that reveals the nature of Satan's development of lawlessness in our nation, is found in the verses I quoted at the beginning of this chapter. I will first examine II Thessalonians 2:1-3: **"Concerning the coming of our Lord Jesus Christ and our being gathered to him, we ask you, brothers, not to become easily unsettled or alarmed by some prophecy, report or letter supposed to have come from us, saying that the day of the Lord has already come. Don't let anyone deceive you in any way, for that day will not come** (he is talking about the return of Jesus) **until the rebellion occurs and the man of lawlessness is revealed, the man doomed to destruction."**

Paul's opening statement, **"Concerning the coming of our Lord Jesus Christ and our being gathered to him,"** indicates that he is talking about the last days, the times in which we are now living.

Paul then says there are two things that must happen before Jesus will return. He says first the rebellion must occur, and second, the man of lawlessness must be revealed.

The Greek word Paul used in this verse for rebellion is *apostasia*. It means to defect or fall into apostasy. To fall into apostasy is to abandon or renounce a belief in following the standards of biblical Christianity. We may wrap ourselves up in the act of religious service, but by our lifestyle we reveal that we no longer are committed to the standards of Christ. This is the type of rebellion Paul is referring to.

In using the word apostasy, Paul is not implying that dedicated Christians won't make their share of mistakes. That is not his point! He knows that will happen. By using the word apostasy he is warning that in the last days, many who go by the name of "Christian" will fall away from being committed to following true biblical standards.

Paul continues his prophetic warning in the third verse by calling those who fall away or rebel against following the biblical standards of God—**"the man of lawlessness."** In modern English a more suitable phrase might be to call such a person a "lawless man." The reason Paul uses the phrase **"man of lawlessness"** is because from a biblical viewpoint anyone who does not respect the laws of God is a person with a lawless spirit.

The spirit of lawlessness Paul warns us about must develop in a society of strong Christian teaching. Otherwise, how can there be a "falling away" from Christian standards, as he points out, if the prominent standards being followed by that society were not there in the first place? The only way you fall from something is if you were already there.

Paul established in verse one that he is talking about the last days—the second coming of Jesus. It is also a well-known fact that America has been the center of Christian activity in these last days. Our country was established on many of the Christian principles found in the Bible. Our constitution was based on Christian standards. In the past we were referred to as a Christian nation. "In God we trust," is written on our money. The majority of American people used Christian standards to live by until recent years.

But in this last generation that all began to change. Our society started to move away from following many of the Christian standards taught in the Bible. Rebellion against God's laws began to take hold. The spirit of lawlessness in man began to take over and change the laws that govern our land. This has developed "a lawless spirit" towards the standards of God in the American people. That is why so many Americas now have the attitude that they have the right to decide right from wrong for themselves. Our nation has moved from honoring God's standards on how we should live, to a point where the majority of people now rely on their own personal judgment to decide proper living standards. That is literally taking the place of God.

We are the only society in the world today that meets the full description of Paul's prophetic warning of a people in the end-times who followed God's standards, then rebelled against His standards. Therefore, we can conclude that his warning must apply to the United States as much or more so than to any other country.

In the next verse, verse 4, Paul tells us how Satan develops this spirit of rebellion or lawlessness against God's standards in the minds of the people in our country. It states: **"He** (which refers to the man with a lawless spirit) **opposes and exalts himself** (his own being) **over everything that is called God or is worshiped, and even sets himself up in God's temple, proclaiming himself to be God."**

It is important to see that the pronoun "himself" occurs three times in this verse. That is the key! It defines **the method of**

seduction that has brought about the rebellion or apostasy from Christian standards that Paul mentions in verse 3.

This verse reveals the spiritual reason why the people of our society have developed a spirit of lawlessness against God's standards in this last generation. It has swept across our nation like a flood. It has been a process of man setting himself up—good ole' me, myself, and I—to decide right from wrong and serving himself as though he was a god.

The Bible says Satan had this same attitude and this is why God cast him out of heaven. Speaking of Satan, God's Word states, **"You said in your heart, I will ascend to heaven; I will raise my throne above the stars of God; I will sit enthroned on the mount of assembly, on the utmost heights of the sacred mountain. I will ascend above the tops of the clouds; I will make myself like the Most High"** (Isaiah 14:13-14). "I," "I," "I," I will do this, I will do that. I will be my own god. That is rebellion! That is lawlessness! It is how in verse 4, Paul describes the **"man of lawlessness,"** he speaks of in verse 3. And he is not talking about just one man; there is more than just one person who rebels and falls. He is addressing the general state of apostasy from Christian standards that takes place in the central area of Christianity in the last days.

This prophetic warning from Paul is powerful! It gives insight to the question many people have been seeking an answer to in the Christian community! Why have the moral values in our country crumbled? Where have we gone wrong? That question is answered in this same verse. We are guilty of setting ourselves up to make our own moral decisions as though we were a god just as Paul prophesied. We are guilty of doing the same thing Satan did in saying, **"I will make myself like the Most High"** (Isaiah 14:14).

In essence that is what Paul is saying in verse 4. I will quote this verse again, **"He** (which refers to the lawless man in verse 3) **opposes and exalts himself** (his own being) **over everything that is called God or is worshiped, and even sets himself up in God's temple, proclaiming himself to be God."** Where does he say man sets himself up? In the temple of God. Where is the temple of God in Christianity? Scripture tells us it is man's body.

"Don't you know that you yourselves are God's temple and that God's Spirit lives in you?" (I Corinthians 3:16).

"Do you not know that your body is a temple of the Holy Spirit, who is in you, whom you have received from God?" (I Corinthians 6:19).

"What agreement is there between the temple of God and idols? For we are the temple of the living God" (II Corinthians 6:16).

There are some that have thought Paul's use of the word "temple" in verse 4 is referring to the temple in Jerusalem. In order to be sure he was talking about the human body, I did a word study on Paul's use of this word and found he was talking about the human body, not the temple in Jerusalem.

There are two Greek words in Scripture that are translated to mean "temple." One is **hieron** and usually refers to the temple in Jerusalem. The other is **naos** and sometimes refers to the heart of the temple in Jerusalem, but when used in Christianity, **naos** is always the Greek word that refers to mankind as being the temple of God.

For example, in all three of the verses I previously quoted from Corinthians which state that the body of man is the temple of God, the Greek word **naos** is used for temple in each verse. The same is true where Jesus says, **"'Destroy this temple** (the Greek word used is naos), **and I will raise it again in** three days.' The Jews replied, 'It has taken forty-six years to build this temple, and you are going to raise it in three days?' But the temple he had spoken of was his body" (John 2:19-21). When the human body is referred to as the temple of God throughout the New Testament, you will find the Greek word **naos** is always used for "temple."

In II Thessalonians 2:1-4, Paul is warning people living in the last days of a rebellion that will take place. The cause of the rebellion is that man sets himself up in the temple of God and serves himself as though he is a god. In verse 4 he used the Greek word **naos** (not **hieron**) for "temple," which means he is talking about the human body, not the temple in Jerusalem. Paul is writing to Christians, and in Christianity mankind is the temple.

I have visited other countries and reviewed how people serve false gods. They do not serve themselves as though they were their own god. They make great personal sacrifices to these false gods.

Our society has developed tremendous resources through our electronic media—TV, the Internet, movies, and press— giving it tremendous power to influence us to accept worldly standards and to decide right from wrong for ourselves. These elements are something the Christian community has never had to contend with before this last generation, and they have created a powerful temptation for everyone to "serve themselves as a god" as never before.

Though the majority of people in our country once respected and lived by the laws of God, many have now rebelled and developed a lawless spirit towards God's laws. We have discarded many biblical moral standards that were once considered normal and have placed our own self interests above our regard for God's laws. This has been done so our own personal desires can be served. We have set ourselves up in the temple of God—the human body—proclaiming ourselves—by the way we serve ourselves—to be god.

II Thessalonians 2:4 is a perfect description of the religion of humanism and the new age movement. It has swept through our country in recent years and has now become the main philosophy that is taught in our schools and is used to establish the standards by which the majority of people live.

Using the powerful influence of our society to serve ourselves like a "god," above the true God, Satan has seduced and deceived the American Christian. To serve ourselves as though we were a god above the true God fits Paul's description of **"the man of lawlessness."**

This warning from Paul tells us that the most important things you and I need to be concerned about in spiritual warfare are not the open and blatant sins we see taking place. Christians are being seduced and deceived in our society to serve themselves above what is normal. That is the trick Satan is using. He is tempting us by appealing to a basic need or by attracting us to something that appears good and legitimate. He won't usually try to tempt us to engage in some gross sin that we can easily detect. He is too smart for that! However, we can be assured he is going to set his traps in his endeavor to get us to fall; you can count on that! *Deception is the way seducing spirits work.*

Jesus gives us our clue on this subject in His warning about the last days by comparing them to Noah and Lot's day (Luke 17:26-30). You will recall I pointed out in chapter one an amazing thing about this list that Jesus gives us; there is not one sin on it. In Noah's day there was violence such as the world had never seen—gross immorality, homosexuality, and many other sins—but Jesus doesn't mention any of those things. The people were eating, drinking (but he doesn't mention drunkenness), marrying, buying, selling, planting, and building. These are all good, legitimate things.

Why does Jesus focus only on the good, legitimate things people were doing in Noah's day? Why didn't He mention our present day immorality, crime, violence, the drug epidemic, overcrowded jails, homosexuality, or abortion? Because He had a greater concern. It is the same as in the days of Noah, the people got caught up and became so engrossed in those things that pertained to their everyday life that they began to serve themselves like a god and neglect the standards of God. That is lawlessness. Their commitment to these things that Jesus mentions caused the people's hearts to grow so cold that they could not hear the message of God's coming judgment. He says the same will be true in our day.

By putting the comments of Jesus and Paul together, we learn that we may be doing good and legitimate things. But if we become so committed to these things that we use them to serve ourselves like a "god," they become bait for the enemy to use to cause us to be disobedient and fall away.

One of the greatest ways we can dishonor the Lord is to put Him in a secondary place in our life. It is a slap in God's face to allow the things of the world to become more important to us than being obedient in carrying out His will and seeking to follow His standards. Paul warns that we need to change our way of thinking because it can lead us into apostasy. That is the substance of what he is saying in this prophetic warning about the last days.

God has equipped every reborn Christian with the power of the Holy Spirit to fulfill our responsibility of being faithful to His standards. Look at these Scriptures:

"You, dear children, are from God and have overcome them, because the one who is in you is greater than the one who is in the world" (I John 4:4).

"...in all these things we are more than conquerors through him who loved us" (Romans 8:37).

"No temptation has seized you except what is common to man. And God is faithful; he will not let you be tempted beyond what you can bear. But when you are tempted, he will also provide a way out so that you can stand up under it" (I Corinthians 10:13).

SIGN OF THE TIMES: CHARACTER

5

In writing to Timothy, the Apostle Paul prophesied about the character of Christians in the last days. He said: **"But mark this: There will be terrible times in the last days. People will be lovers of themselves, lovers of money, boastful, proud, abusive, disobedient to their parents, ungrateful, unholy** (immoral), **without love, unforgiving, slanderous, without self-control, brutal, not lovers of the good, treacherous, rash, conceited, lovers of pleasure rather than lovers of God—having a form of godliness but denying its power. Have nothing to do with them"** (II Timothy 3:1-5).

Paul lists several characteristics of the heart in these verses, which have become so much a part of the character of Christians in these last days, that he referred to our day as **"terrible times."**

We are seeing this prophecy come true. Christians in America have lost their ability to overcome many of the sins mentioned in these verses. We are no longer people with clean hands and pure hearts with our affections set on things above. Divorce, immorality, dishonesty and greed run rampant in the church. No longer are we willing to sacrifice our self-serving lifestyle to seek God's standards first. The moral structure of our society is collapsing, and we have done little to **stand firm** and **fight** against the problem.

In this last generation, the availability of so many things of the world has created a temptation for Christians, which is unprecedented in the history of mankind. It is beyond one's imagination. It has become nearly impossible for most people to avoid falling into at least some of Satan's worldly traps. It has changed the moral character of God's people as Paul describes in these verses in his letter to Timothy.

We need look no further than ourselves to find the real reason behind the corruption and violence in our nation. Our hearts are no longer in tune with the heart of God. This is what has brought about the bitter harvest of suffering and defeat that we are experiencing in our country today. As stated earlier we have allowed Satan to undermine our families, our public schools, our government, our way of thinking, and our social order. Violence, immorality, and the tragedies they cause are now taking a heavy toll on the American people.

We have allowed Satan to exchange our commitment to righteousness for a spirit of tolerance towards the ways of the world. This is reflected by the characteristics of the heart Paul writes about. They reveal that the body of Christ in our day has developed what I call an epidemic of, *"spiritual heart disease."*

Jesus said, **"For where your treasure is, there your heart will be also"** (Matthew 6:21). And, **"...the things that come out of the mouth come from the heart, and these make a man 'unclean.' For out of the heart come evil thoughts, murder, adultery, sexual immorality, theft, false testimony, slander"** (Matthew 15:18-19). **"The heart is deceitful above all things..."** (Jeremiah 17:9). It is what comes out of "the heart" that reveals our character, and Satan knows that is where we are most vulnerable. He is out to win the battle for control over the hearts of as many Christians in America as possible.

To explain what I mean by *"spiritual heart disease"* I will illustrate by discussing *"physical heart disease."*

"Physical heart disease" is the leading cause of death in the United States. More than one million Americans suffer a heart attack every year. Nearly half of all deaths in this country each year result from cardiovascular disease. Over 60 million Americans have one or more forms of heart disease. Every minute of every day, three Americans have heart attacks. Heart disease is the worst plague America has ever known. Besides taking so many lives, it also costs the American people over 100 billion dollars each year to treat, which includes the expense of physician and nursing services, hospital and nursing home care, medications and lost productivity. Yet, many people throughout the world are not plagued with heart disease. Death from heart disease is virtually unknown in many countries.

"Physical heart disease" (arteriosclerosis) is the hardening of the arteries. It is the accumulation of "plaque" in the circulatory system. As plaque accumulates on the walls of the arteries, they become narrow and consequently the flow of blood to the body's vital organs is restricted. This build-up of plaque hardens and narrows arteries, which leads to restricted flow of blood, blood clots, heart attacks, and death. If a clot occurs in one of the coronary arteries—the channels that supply the heart with life-sustaining blood—a heart attack results. The accumulation of plaque within the arteries is one of the most dangerous, unhealthy (often deadly) things that can happen to the human body.

"Spiritual heart disease" is the term I use to indicate the hardening of our spiritual arteries. A disease that hinders the flow of the Holy Spirit in our inner being, something that is necessary to develop in us the true righteousness of God.

It is a known fact that the build-up of *"plaque"* in the arteries of our physical bodies is extremely dangerous. In a similar way, the Bible teaches that a build-up of love and attachment to what Scripture calls **"anything in the world"** will become *"spiritual plaque"* to the Christian and will be just as dangerous to our spiritual growth and commitment.

This is why there is so much in Scripture that warns us about the things of the world or human society. For example, **"Do not love the world or anything in the world. If anyone loves the world, the love of the Father is not in him"** (I John 2:15). **"Religion that God our Father accepts as pure and faultless is this: to look after orphans and widows in their distress and to keep oneself from being polluted by the world"** (James 1:27). **"You adulterous people, don't you know that friendship with the world is hatred toward God? Anyone who chooses to be a friend of the world becomes an enemy of God"** (James 4:4). **"As for you, you were dead in your transgressions and sins, in which you used to live when you followed the ways of this world..."** (Ephesians 2:1-2a).

The key phase is: **"Do not love the world or anything in the world"** which means do not become committed or attached to "the things of the world." Instead we are to be **"...the light of the world"** (Matthew 5:14). Or as Jesus said, **"If you belonged to the world, it would love you as its own. As it is, you do not belong to the world, but I have chosen you out of the world..."** (John 15:19).

73

Contrary to what we may think, this phrase **"anything in the world"** in Scripture, does not necessarily refer to material possessions. In Scripture, the word **"world"** has three primary meanings. **First,** it refers to the material universe (including the Earth) as in Matthew 13:35. **Second,** "world" refers to the inhabitants of the Earth, or mankind, as in John 3:16. **Third,** "world" is used to mean the moral and spiritual systems, which bonds humans together otherwise known as *"human society."*

It is the **third** meaning of the word **"world"** in the phrase **"anything in the world"** that functions like *"spiritual plaque."* In other words, if we become attached or overcommitted in our hearts to the things of *"human society,"* they will harden us towards the righteousness of God.

To know exactly what *"spiritual plaque"* consists of, we will define this term. It is that realm of the world developed by the efforts of mankind rather than created by God. It consists of man-made religions; political structures and governments; economic, business, and financial systems; educational systems; science and technology; along with entertainment and amusements. Eliminate these things and you eliminate society; they make up what is referred to in Scripture as **"anything in the world."**

These verses do not mean we can't use *"the things of the world"* or we can't be involved in *"the things of the world."* We are not to become attached, overcommitted to, in love with— *"the things of society."* This would apply not only to material possessions, but business, education, religion, entertainment, sports, etc. All of these things can be used by the enemy to harden our hearts towards placing the things of God first. We are to be *"in"* the world (society) but not *"of"* the world. Jesus said, **"...they are not of the world any more than I am of the world. My prayer is not that you take them out** of the world but that you protect them from the evil one. They are not of the world, even as I am not of it" (John 17:14-16).

If we become overly attached or committed to anything that makes up *"human society"* (the world), that is when it will begin to function as *"spiritual plaque"* and harden our hearts as this reduces the control the Holy Spirit has on our life. We become more tolerant of the ways of the world, apathetic, or indifferent, and will begin to compromise the standards of God.

According to the Word of God, the whole structure of society is ordered by a principle of life that is foreign to God and leads people away from Him. That is because the spiritual power, Satan, governs it from behind the scenes. He is even called the god of this world or society. **"The god of this age** (world) **has blinded the minds of unbelievers"** (II Corinthians 4:4). **"...the whole world** (society) **is under the control of the evil one** (Satan)" (I John 5:19).

Christians usually have no problem understanding that we have been under the bondage of sin. We readily agree that sinful things emanate from Satan. But we do have a problem recognizing that many of the things in society are under the control of Satan. Yet Scripture clearly affirms that to be true.

This is not to say that the things developed by mankind—the things of the world—of society—cannot be removed from the world system and claimed for the glory of God. Just as human beings who are of the world can be converted, so can the things they construct. But we need to recognize God's warning about *"the things of society"* and Satan's control over them. We need to be alert that the enemy uses them as *"spiritual plaque"* to harden our spiritual arteries and stop the flow of our spiritual blood—the power of the Holy Spirit. Satan uses "things of the world" to wage war against our commitment to Jesus and to cause us to commit adultery with the world. That is how he breaks down our commitment to biblical standards, which will eventually change our character.

Satan knows that to try and influence us through activities that are clearly recognizable as sinful will not yield him much success. Instead, he has fabricated an enticing worldly society in our country—called the great society—in which he artfully develops our commitment to **"anything in the world"** *(his spiritual plaque)* to entrap unsuspecting Christians.

The Lord gave Paul spiritual eyes to see into the future. When he saw what is now happening, and its effects on Christians, he wrote to Timothy, **"But mark this: There will be terrible times in the last days"** (II Timothy 3:1). We should make note of the fact that Paul's reaction to our day was similar to the reaction of Jesus. Though he called our day **"terrible times,"** Paul, like Jesus when Jesus was comparing our day to Noah's day, was not referring to the many gross sins that are now happening. The many gross sins in our day was not Paul's main concern. The terrible times he was talking about were the several worldly characteristics he foresaw becoming common in Christians during the last days. Those are the characteristics he listed and I quoted at the beginning of this chapter from II Timothy 3:2-4.

At the end of his list Paul says, **"having a form of godliness but denying its power."** Living a Christian life without the power of God is evident by the way we live our daily lives. Not one of these characteristics in Paul's list are of God. If they are controlling our nature it is because we have slowed, or stopped, the flow of the Holy Spirit as our power source in overcoming the characteristics and ways of the world.

The temptations coming out of the world system that are designed by our enemy to cause us to quench the power of the Holy Spirit in our life are so enticing and strong. Their ability to get us to commit over and above what is normal to the many *"things of the world"* is overwhelming at times. In today's environment it is so easy to overextend ourselves and get caught up in sin by cheating, being dishonest, greedy, or immoral and allowing these characteristics Paul lists to control our actions.

It is my prayer that you are beginning to see why God's main concern about the days in which we live is more than just the many evil sins that are taking place. As I have tried to explain, it is also how His people have become so involved in the affairs of this life that we are not paying any attention to His warnings of a coming judgment if we do not change our ways. According to Scripture this concerns God more than anything. He knows how devastating this will be for so many people if they are not prepared should He have to judge our society.

Why does the Lord bring judgment? It is because we allow deception to take root in our hearts and control our minds to the point where we become misguided and careless in living a godly life. God's judgment is His way of correcting the elements that the enemy uses to lead us astray from serving, loving and worshiping only God. Any judgment carried out by God is for our spiritual benefit. It is not for Him. It only brings pain to His heart. But He loves us too much to let us continue on a path of spiritual apathy.

To become Christ-like in the characteristics of our heart is one of the key objectives throughout the life of Christians in their spiritual development. The list of worldly characteristics Paul saw in the lives of Christians in our time tells us how lacking the development of true Christian characteristics have been among Christians in this last generation. I am going to name, and briefly describe those characteristics that controlled the heart of Jesus. Notice how opposite they are compared to those listed by Paul in his letter to Timothy.

Jesus himself taught the following Christian characteristics of the heart in the greatest sermon ever preached, "The Sermon on The Mount." These are the true characteristics He wants to develop in those who follow Him.

Each one of these Christian characteristics focus on and deal with the heart. The heart is where our commitment must originate in true Christianity. I doubt if any one of these characteristics of Jesus is fully obtainable over the lifetime of our spiritual development. But they are to be what we set our eyes on and our commitment towards, as we develop spiritually. They are the mirrors for us to examine ourselves. They are quite different from the teachings of the world.

Following are the general characteristics of the Christian faith. Notice that each one carries a promise or blessing of happiness.

Characteristic Number One: **"Blessed** (happy) **are the poor in spirit, for theirs is the kingdom of heaven"** (Matthew 5:3).

Jesus was poor in spirit. He was devoid of any self-interest. It is the key to all that follows in the development of our Christian walk. This characteristic deals with the emptying of our self-will, our self-serving nature, and being filled with God's nature through the power of His Holy Spirit.

The world system promotes "self-assertion," "self-satisfaction," "self-exaltation," and "self-glorification." It emphasizes personalities, natural abilities, appearance, family heritage, nationality, natural temperaments, intelligence, wealth, worldly position and authority. The world system despises this quality of "poor in spirit" that was a part of the character of Jesus.

The characteristics of Jesus opposed practically every teaching you will find in the world. It was because His character was in such direct conflict with the ways of the world that the people of His day wanted to get rid of Him. They wanted Him out of their sight. They hated His character. They did not know how to deal with it. So they tried to shoot out His light by crucifying Him. They did not realize that the character of one's heart couldn't be destroyed through death.

We cannot develop this characteristic of "poor in spirit" by using our own will power. It is impossible. The same is true for any of the characteristics of Jesus. Even if we tried to use our own will power, we would probably have to remove ourselves from society. We may even endeavor to change our personality by purposely bringing about some personal hardship. But this or any other type of activity on our part will only end up making us less "poor in spirit" because it will only create a greater awareness of "self." Any of these Christian characteristics taught by Jesus can only be developed by the power of the Holy Spirit. That is why it is so critical that He gains greater and greater control of our hearts. A process which virtually comes to a halt when we become attached, fall in love with, **...anything in the world...** (I John 2:15), because an attachment to the things of the world will develop into *spiritual plaque.*

Christian Characteristic Number Two: **"Blessed** (happy) **are those who mourn, for they will be comforted"** (Matthew 5:4).

This is another characteristic of the heart, which is totally contrary to the teachings of society. Jesus mourned because He saw the effects of sin on the human race and the world as it really is. He did not try to escape from reality.

This characteristic of mourning is something most people run from. They try to avoid it altogether. It is amazing to consider all of the energy, enthusiasm and expense the world system uses through worldly pleasure and entertainment to blind us to the effects of sin and to move us away from developing "the spirit of mourning."

Jesus saw the harm this horrid, ugly and foul thing called sin did to the people. He saw its terrible results! It causes pain, sickness, grief, distress and unhappiness, in addition to sending people to the grave on their way to Hell.

The reason Jesus mourned is because He saw what sin does to people. He also knew sin stabs God right in the heart. He knew how much pain sin has caused God, both for what it does to people and the fact that it was the reason God had to send Jesus to suffer and die on the cross.

This characteristic of mourning will help open our eyes to see the spiritual needs of mankind. The degree to which we possess this characteristic plays heavily on our appreciation of the deep love God has for us and the commitment we will make to live the Christian way of life.

Christian Characteristic Number Three: **"Blessed** (happy) **are the meek, for they will inherit the earth"** (Matthew 5:5).

This is another characteristic of the heart where Jesus brings us face to face with something completely opposite to the natural thinking of mankind.

For Jesus to imply that "the meek shall inherit the earth" baffled the wisdom of the world. Our natural way of thinking is to control and influence the world by relying on the strength and power of the military, material goods, intellect and aggressiveness.

Jesus did not try to accomplish the things of God through man's ability. He submitted Himself and His will completely to

God, being totally committed and dependent on Him and His power. Examples of other people who developed this characteristic of meekness in their life were Moses, David, Abraham, the prophets, Paul, Peter as well as many other men and women throughout the history of God's people.

Through the life of Jesus we can see that meekness does not mean being flabby, or lacking in strength, firmness, vigor or force. Jesus was not easy-going, weak in personality, nor did He exhibit a compromising spirit of peace at any price. He knew His mission and set His face as a flint to accomplish it.

People talked about Him, scorned Him, stated untruths about Him, denied Him His rightful position, privileges, possessions and status in life, and did not allow Him the right to express His opinion. It was this characteristic of meekness that caused Him not to demand His personal rights or position. He was a vessel for God to live in and through, and it was God's will and purpose He sought and lived for—not His own purpose.

The apostle Paul also demonstrated the characteristic of meekness, as he grew older. If he were alive today, he would probably hold a Ph.D. in philosophy and theology. He would have a working knowledge of economics, political science, history and languages; he spoke several languages. He was a devoted religious man, zealous in his commitment to a religious system as a member of the Pharisee sect. I am sure he fasted a couple of times a week, prayed three times a day, gave ten percent of his earnings and seldom missed attending the assembly. By the standards of the world he had a long list of personal credentials.

But with all his religion, political authority, economic position, educational background and intellectual ability Paul said, **"If anyone else thinks he has reasons to put confidence in the flesh** (natural abilities), **I have more:...But whatever** was to my profit I now consider loss for the sake of Christ. **What is more, I consider everything a loss compared to the surpassing greatness of knowing Christ Jesus my Lord, for whose sake I have lost all things. I consider them rubbish, that I may gain Christ and be found in him, not having a righteousness of my own that comes from the law, but that which is through faith in Christ—the righteousness that comes from God and is by faith"** (Philippians 3:4b, 7-9).

Paul lost all confidence in his natural ability. That is the characteristic of meekness. It allowed God to accomplish more through Paul than anyone else in early church history. He wrote more books in the New Testament than anyone, and his several missionary journeys became a part of Scripture.

We may not become a great spiritual leader like Moses, Paul, or Peter. Even if that were God's purpose for us, it took the Lord many years to develop these godly characteristics in these individuals before they could completely accomplish the will of God in their lives. To fulfill God's will for our life we first must humble ourselves (demonstrate this characteristic of meekness) and surrender our will completely to the Lord. This characteristic of meekness will then grow to become a part of our heart and our daily commitment.

Christian Characteristic Number Four: **"Blessed** (happy) **are those who hunger and thirst for righteousness, for they will be filled"** (Matthew 5:6).

One of the major areas that distinguished Jesus from all other people who ever lived is that He never sinned. He had a hunger and thirst for righteousness and He was filled.

To "hunger and thirst" is to have a deep and desperate need. It is the feeling one has if away from home for a long time and then becomes homesick. We become so desperate it hurts.

This characteristic in our heart will develop an inner nature that desperately seeks the righteous nature of God. It is this heart characteristic that testifies of our commitment to obedience.

This characteristic carries with it a promise that we will be filled. It will not be through our efforts, but through the power of God's grace. Jesus said, **"But seek first his kingdom and his righteousness, and all these things will be given to you..."** (Matthew 6:33). Righteousness is the way to real peace.

Notice that Jesus did not hunger and thirst after happiness or blessings because they are a natural consequence of seeking righteousness. If what we seek is the wrong thing, the end result will be like a doctor treating the pain and ignoring the cause.

Christian Characteristic Number Five: **"Blessed** (happy) **are the merciful, for they will be shown mercy"** (Matthew 5:7).

The characteristic of mercy in Jesus is what allowed Him to see the miserable consequences of sin. It is what drove Him to act and relieve the suffering sin causes both in this life and life after death in Hell. Mercy caused Him to have a deep sense of pity, compassion and sorrow for mankind.

Mercy allowed Jesus to see people with a different eye. It is why He made the proper distinction between the sin and the sinner. He saw people as creatures that are slaves to sin on their way to Hell—as creatures who needed forgiveness—and He desired to do something about it.

The characteristic of mercy develops a sacrificial love for mankind, a caring love that inspires a person to do all he or she can to save another from the fiery pits of Hell.

We can be so thankful we have a merciful God. He knows the consequences of sin. Mercy is what caused Him to have pity on mankind and take action to save us. The characteristic of mercy not only sees the need, it causes us to take action and do something about the need. The Bible says: **"For God so loved the world** (mankind) **that he gave his one and only Son** (Jesus Christ), **that whoever believes in him** (accepts Him in their heart as their Savior) **shall not perish** (spend eternity in Hell) **but have eternal life** (will spend eternity in Heaven). **For God did not send his Son** (Jesus Christ) **into the world to condemn the world, but to save the world through him. Whoever believes in him** (accepts Jesus in their heart as their Savior) **is not condemned, but whoever does not believe stands condemned already because he has not believed in the name of God's one and only Son** (Jesus Christ)" (John 3:16-18).

Mercy differentiates between the sinner and sin. God hates sin but loves the sinner. Mercy changes our attitude toward others. It causes us to begin to see people as creatures to be pitied—creatures who are slaves to sin—creatures who have been trapped and engulfed in Satan's world system and who are suffering the awful consequences of sin.

After He had been beaten and was hanging on the cross being crucified, mercy moved Jesus to say, **"Father, forgive them, for they do not know what they are doing"** (Luke 23:34). It was this characteristic of mercy in His heart that allowed Jesus to see through those who persecuted Him. He could see that they were victims of Satan and his world system.

His mercy and love for mankind is what drove Jesus to live a sinless life so that He could fulfill His mission and be the perfect sacrifice for the sins of mankind and save us from going to Hell. Our going to Heaven was far more important to Him than His own personal welfare.

Christian Characteristic Number Six: **"Blessed** (happy) **are the pure in heart, for they will see God"** (Matthew 5:8).

The single most important motivation behind all that Jesus did was to love, serve and glorify God rather than serve Himself. He exemplified the characteristic of being "pure in heart."

This characteristic deals with the cause of all of mankind's problems. **"For out of the heart,"** Jesus said, **"come evil thoughts..."** (Matthew 15:19). Any problem or unworthy desire in life always stems from the heart.

The whole foundation of Christian doctrine as lived and taught by Jesus emphasizes having a pure heart. We need to be changed from the inside out and receive a new heart because by nature we do not have a pure heart.

To be "pure in heart" means freedom from hypocrisy. Hypocrisy may be the worst of all heart problems because it is a lie within our heart that has an attractive cover to hide the truth. It causes us to be dishonest, insincere and to deceive ourselves.

A hypocritical heart will try to hide sin and its effects. It thinks only of the pleasure of the moment. A sincere heart is willing to reveal sin and the truth of its ultimate consequences.

The hypocrite may even claim a share in Christ and His righteousness. He might be involved in religious activity and may appear to outdo the committed Christian. But God looks at the heart, He knows better. Judas confidently sat down with the apostles at Passover as if he were the most welcome, holiest guest of all, yet his heart was evil and he eventually betrayed Christ.

We need to be sincere about our commitment to Christianity. We must not speak about a personal relationship with Jesus Christ, when in our heart it is not true.

Job had a "pure heart." The Bible tells us that Satan muddied up Job's life, but Job's spirit continued to flow from an honest heart before God. We need to be careful that we don't make a false profession of our spiritual state. Thinking that we are one place spiritually and actually being in another place can be a very harmful deception of the heart.

David was called a *"man after God's own heart"* because in his heart, there was no spirit of deceit. Yes, he was deceived and he fell, but he had no "spirit of deceit" which is to have a hypocritical heart. He had a "pure heart!" This was reflected because when his spiritual eyes were opened he quickly was willing to confess the sin he had committed.

The key was the reaction of David's heart. He did not try to excuse or hide his sin. He knew he had done wrong and was ready for God's judgment. Because of his "purity of heart," David was quick to fully repent before the Lord and did not fall out of favor with God when he did wrong. However, he did suffer many terrible consequences in his life because of the sins he had committed.

King David is a good example of the awful pain and heartache that sin causes in this life. Because of his repentant heart and confession before God, he was not prevented from spending eternal life in Heaven. However, the pleasure of his sin for a short season brought him nothing but terrible misery for the last 20 years of his life on Earth.

To allow the Lord to develop in us a new pure heart is critical to the Christian walk of life. It will bring with it a singleness of mind to seek God's holiness, His pure love, and a genuine faith that will truly reflect the evidence of Christ in our lives.

It is a "pure heart" that is ready for spiritual responsibility because this heart is merged with God's will. Even when our best effort fails, the willingness of a pure heart means success to God.

Christian Characteristic Number Seven: **"Blessed (happy) are the peacemakers, for they will be called sons of God"** (Matthew 5:9).

Jesus' mission was to be a vessel that brought peace on Earth and goodwill to all men. What a beautiful characteristic it is to be a peacemaker! Of all aspirations inner peace is the one thing that mankind strives the most to possess.

As a peacemaker, Jesus was not a person who kept quiet just to avoid trouble or to appease others all the time. It was this characteristic that allowed Him to be absolutely neutral when surrounded by conflict and to be totally free from defensiveness and hypersensitivity. His sole interest was to bring inner peace to mankind regardless of the personal sacrifice required. He saw a larger, more important purpose in life than protecting His personal rights. That is why He was able to go to the cross to provide the hope of peace in our hearts.

As a peacemaker, Jesus viewed all disputes, whether between individuals or nations, as distractions that detracted from the glory of God. He was selfless, loving and approachable. Other people could sense that He was a peacemaker and could approach Him knowing they would receive understanding and direction that would give them peace in their hearts.

What a contrast between those worldly characteristics we quoted earlier that Paul spoke of in his letter to Timothy and these seven characteristics, which are the guiding characteristics of Christianity as given by Jesus!

These characteristics of Christ tell us we cannot control our Christianity. Our Christianity is meant to control us through the power of the Holy Spirit. We soon discover that *being* is more important than *doing.* This is why *"spiritual plaque"* is so harmful to the character and spiritual growth of a Christian. It stops the flow of the power of the Holy Spirit in our lives. When this happens, our heart is controlled by the worldly characteristics Paul mentions, rather than by the spiritual characteristics given by Jesus. This explains why Paul ends the list of worldly characteristics that he saw dominating Christians in the last days by saying we **"have a form of godliness but deny its power."**

There is only a limited amount of teaching heard these days on the seven characteristics of a Christian as taught by Jesus in "The Sermon on the Mount." God's warning about Christian character, as a sign of the times, is very valid for our day.

I have discussed five different "signs of the times" so you can see why God's judgment could come on America if we do not change our life style. I reviewed a direct warning from Jesus, economics, lawlessness, seducing spirits, and Christian character. We will next look at some guiding principles about how to prepare for God's judgment if we don't change our ways enough to prevent it.

BE PREPARED

6

Please take a moment to ask yourself the following question: "what should I do to be prepared for God's judgment should it come?" The thought that will usually come to mind is: "what should I do physically?" That is normal and makes good sense. Most of us will think of some practical suggestions and they are important, but we need more than that! We need to know the mind of the Lord in these trying times. Everybody's situation is different so we need guidelines or principles to follow that will apply or work for everyone.

To "Prepare Yourself" so that your physical needs are met if God's judgment should come, there is only one way to be assured this will happen. You must first follow the principles taught in the Bible, which are to "Prepare Yourself" spiritually.

If we are going to be led by the Lord in a way for Him to meet our physical needs, spiritual preparation is the key. It was the key to Noah's success during God's judgment in his day; it was the key to those in Israel who saw their needs met when God had to judge Israel; and it will be the key to our success if God's judgment falls on America. It has been that way since the beginning of mankind. The Lord has always been faithful in meeting the needs of those who are faithfully following Him and His ways.

FEAR NOT THE DAYS TO COME, BUT FEAR THIS ONLY: THAT YOU SHALL WALK IN A MANNER PLEASING TO THE LORD. This is the commitment Christians need to make to prepare for our troubled world. It is the theme for the message in this book.

It is important for you to see the need to "Prepare Yourself" spiritually so that you will be ready should God's judgment come on America. Because then, and only then, can you know that the Lord will supply all of your needs, regardless of the circumstances that may develop.

The fruits of most Christians in America reveal that we are not prepared for the warning Jesus gave about our times. We are not prepared for God's warning about the economic temptations that have strangled many of us. We are not prepared to handle God's warning about seducing spirits that have deceived us into accepting many of the world's standards. We are not prepared for God's warning about the lawless spirit that has exploded across the central area of Christianity. We are not prepared for God's warning about how all of this would cause worldly characteristics to become commonplace in the lives of many Christians.

Many Americans, Christians included, have become wrapped up in self-seeking pursuits and careless living. This has led to an even greater danger—an overall lack of respect for the standards of God. This was a major aspect of spiritual deterioration in Noah's day, and according to Scripture, it is a great concern for God today. It brought down God's judgment in the past, and as we examine some of the things that are happening in our country today, it is becoming more and more apparent that in some ways "God's hedge of protection has already begun to be lifted over America." Few Christians are prepared!

Any Christian willing to face reality must admit that we are in serious trouble. What was unthinkable a generation ago has now become commonplace. The moral fiber that bound our nation and our people together for centuries has unraveled.

• **The family, the most fundamental means of preserving social order, has been shattered.**

• **Greed and unethical conduct have tainted professions (doctors, bankers, lawyers, politicians, educators, some spiritual leaders, etc.) who have historically represented the "pillars of society."**

• **Crime and violence stalk America's great cities, once the principle evidence of a mighty, industrial nation.**

• **Sexual immorality and life styles devoted to self-gratification have transformed the American character.**

• **Public schools, once the showpiece of a young democracy, have surrendered to drug abuse, sex, and criminal violence.**

• **Our government has turned its back on the scriptural principles that formed the moral foundation of America by passing immoral laws.**

• **Americans have reserved their most vicious attack for children through abortion and child abuse.**

America has discarded the biblical standards on which our nation was founded as fast as yesterday's news. *"If you can get away with it, then it is all right"* has become the slogan of many people. As a result, our culture has sanctioned the murder of over 40 million babies by abortion as an exercise in personal freedom. In reality this has been the witness of a ghastly sacrifice of human life to the god of "self." Abortion should be an eye opening illustration of the self-serving spirit that has swept across our land in this last generation.

91

The rotten fruit produced by our society is there for all to see, and Jesus said that we could know the health of a plant by looking at its fruit. There is no excuse for any Christian to be uninformed. We cannot afford to allow the enemy to continue to blind us. Because, as it was in the days of Noah, we too can be so caught up in the everyday affairs of our life that we can't hear and won't believe the possibility that God's judgment is coming on America if we do not change our ways. How are we going to survive these last hours if we are not prepared as was Noah?

If our day is similar to the days of Noah, which Jesus says they are, then one of our best sources for gaining information about preparing for God's judgment is to review the attitude and activities of Noah. Hebrews 11:7 gives us some vital insights that will help us in our preparation.

"By faith Noah, when warned about things not yet seen, in holy fear built an ark to save his family" (Hebrews 11:7).

The **first** thing that motivated Noah to prepare himself and his family was "his faith." He believed God's warning! Before anything else, to prepare ourselves for these last days, we must believe there is a possibility that God's judgment is going to fall as Scripture warns. When? I don't know the exact time. How? I can only speculate. Will I still be alive? I don't know. These things are not the issue. The issue is that before we will accept direction from God and His Word about what we should do to prepare ourselves, we must first believe what God's Word warns us about. All things in our relationship with the Lord begin with our faith. The same truth applies in this situation. If we don't believe that judgment is possible, and that in some areas it has already begun, we won't be willing to step out in faith to follow the Lord's leading in how we should prepare.

The **second** important thing we learn about Noah's preparation is his attitude. After receiving a warning from God, which he believed, he stepped out in faith with an attitude of *"holy fear"* within his character and took action. This is critical! Holy fear is what motivates humans to adhere to God's standards and not give in to worldly standards.

Godly standards had been lost in Noah's day. But possessing a holy fear of God in his character, Noah cultivated a deep reliance on God and a love for God's standards. This verse says of Noah, **"...in holy fear built an ark to save his family."** Walking in holy fear led him to take action to save his family. He trusted in God and His Word completely. His obedience was foremost in his mind because he had a proper fear or respect for the Lord. Since Jesus said our times are similar to Noah's, it will be this same attitude that will help preserve us.

"...Learn to fear the Lord your God..." (Deuteronomy 31:12). **"Let all the earth fear the Lord..."** (Psalm 33:8). **"The angel of the Lord encamps around those who fear him, and He delivers them"** (Psalm 34:7). **"...through the fear of the Lord a man avoids evil"** (Proverbs 16:6). **"To fear the Lord is to hate evil;..."** (Proverbs 8:13). **"...live your lives as strangers here in reverent fear"** (I Peter 1:17). **"Then the church...was strengthened; and encouraged by the Holy Spirit...living in the fear of the Lord"** (Acts 9:31).

These are just a few of the many verses that touch on the subject of having a proper fear of the Lord. To have a "holy fear" is to stand in awe of and have a deep respect for God's holiness and His standards. Possession of this characteristic is what gives us that inner desire to avoid sin. It gives us a conscious desire to avoid anything we are aware of that would displease the Lord. Obedience to Him becomes our utmost priority.

Prepare Yourself

To have a proper holy fear of the Lord means to seek His will in all things—to examine every aspect of what is going on in our life with God's Word. To be in God's will becomes a deep concern and a driving force behind every thought and action.

Holy fear develops the desire to subject everything in our lives to the same exacting standard: *"Is this pleasing to God?"* Holy fear develops a heart that is pure, open to conviction and repentance. It allows the Lord to open our spiritual eyes. **Holy fear gives us discernment.**

To stay in line spiritually, a Christian needs to have a proper fear of the Lord. If we don't, we will take certain spiritual things for granted. We will lose our sensitivity and alertness to the influence of the world around us. We can easily develop spiritual pride and take liberties, which will not only affect our spiritual walk but will hurt others. Without holy fear our heart can quickly become hypocritical in certain areas. We don't have a fear of sinning like we should. We become negligent in seeking righteousness.

Holy fear is needed for a healthy spiritual walk. Jesus always kept His eyes on the mark. He avoided sin at every turn. He never wavered. A proper holy fear will keep us from straying from God's standards and moving towards worldly standards. It will help keep us from being led astray easily by those who have gotten off the track.

To **prepare yourself** for the possibility of God's hand of judgment falling on America will require no less on our part than it did on Noah's part. By faith he believed God and moved with a holy fear to prepare an ark to save his family. A healthy, fearful attitude toward God is a key to being prepared spiritually for judgment.

If your standards as a Christian allow you to walk along the edge of darkness, then it is a sure indication that you don't have the kind of holy fear towards God that Noah had and that Scripture talks about. We must strive to stay as far away as possible from worldly standards and give no advantage to Satan. Our habit of mind must be to have a strong desire to avoid sin at every turn, to walk uprightly in a manner pleasing to Him, and to live in awe of the Lord. This is what it will take to build the ark we need to keep us safe from the pressures, temptations, and trials of our day.

Judgment awaits around the comer. So we must do what Noah did. We must start with a proper fear of the Lord. Those who fear the Lord have nothing to be afraid of from the world in the days to come no matter what happens. That is because in God's family, great courage against the enemy begins with a proper *"fear of the Lord."* According to Scripture, the Lord will protect us regardless of circumstances if we have a healthy *"fear of the Lord."*

In addition to Hebrews 11:7, there are other areas of Scripture I would suggest you seek out and study that inform us about being under God's judgment—Isaiah, chapters 1-5 for example. I do not review these chapters in this book, but I do review them in my book entitled, "Holy Fear."

One other Scripture about judgment I do want to review in this book is II Chronicles 7:13-14. You will hear verse 14 quoted quite often these days. I like to also include verse 13 because these two verses go together in Scripture to make one sentence. **"When I shut up the heavens so that there is no rain, or command locusts to devour the land or send a plague among my people, if my people, who are called by my name, will humble themselves and pray and seek my face and turn from their wicked ways, then will I hear**

from heaven and will forgive their sin and will heal their land" (II Chronicles 7:13-14).

The setting behind these two verses is interesting. They came as a Word from God through Solomon for the Israelites during a time of great prosperity. At the time, they were not under judgment. The conditions then were similar to those in America as I write this book; we are living in a time of great prosperity.

The first part of II Chronicles 7:13-14 definitely speaks of being under God's judgment. Then the second part informs the people of the things they must do when they come under God's judgment. The Word of God does not change. We need to learn these same principles if we are going to **be prepared** for God's coming judgment. I will examine verse 14, which tells us some things we need to know.

"If my people who are called by my name"—this verse is obviously directed to God's people which today would be Christians. It is important to see the Lord's direction in this verse is prefaced with the word **"if."** There are several conditions we must follow before the promise at the end of the verse will be fulfilled.

The **first "if"** condition is: **"will humble themselves."** We might do the other things mentioned in this verse—pray, seek God's face, and turn from our wicked ways—but **"if"** we have not first humbled ourselves, it does not appear the Lord can lift His hand of judgment. You may recall that humility, or meekness, was one of the key heart characteristics Jesus emphasized in His "Sermon on the Mount."

One of God's purposes in bringing judgment upon a person or a nation is to humble them or deal with the pride in their hearts. The characteristic of pride in the American people has definitely become a problem and has made a heavy contribution to the moral conditions we now find in our country. Pride stands in the way of true love, the ability to give of oneself, which is the very nature of God (see I Corinthians 13:4). Pride is the opposite of being broken. A heart God revives is a humble and broken heart. **"The sacrifices of God are a broken spirit; a broken and contrite heart, O God, you will not despise"** (Psalm 51:17). God says, **"...I hate pride and arrogance..."** (Proverbs 8:13). **"Pride only breeds quarrels..."** (Proverbs 13:10). **"The Lord detests all the proud of heart..."** (Proverbs 16:5). **"Before his downfall a man's heart is proud..."** (Proverbs 18:12). **"Live in harmony with one another. Do not be proud, but be willing to associate with people of low position. Do not be conceited"** (Romans 12:16). **"...God opposes the proud but gives grace to the humble"** (James 4:6). Pride has become one of the greatest spiritual problems in the American church.

The **second "if"** condition in II Chronicles 7:14 is to **"Pray"** and the **third** is to **"seek God's face."** There is a lot of good material available about prayer and seeking God's face. It is important that we become well-informed about these two subjects. I suggest you get involved in a good Bible-based study on them both.

The **fourth "if"** condition God required in time of judgment is to **"turn from their wicked ways."** To **"turn from"** means to repent. **"Their wicked ways"** means that God's people must turn from following the ways of the world and seek His righteousness. I have fully discussed this subject throughout the book.

This message in II Chronicles 7:14 was to believers, not to the people of the world. It must be emphasized that in a time of judgment, the Lord is trying to break and separate His people from the sins of the world. There are several things the Lord says we must do to spiritually get our lives back on the right path. We must humble ourselves, pray, seek God's face, repent, and seek God's righteousness. He says **"if"** we will do these things **"...then will I hear from heaven** (hear our prayers) **and will forgive their sin and will heal their land** (bring revival)" (II Chronicles 7:14). For revival to take place, all of these **"if"** conditions need to become a part of our everyday Christian life. I believe this principle would apply to an individual, a church, or even a nation.

God's formula then, for you and me to prepare ourselves for His coming judgment is as follows: <u>First, we must believe God's warning that His judgment hand could fall! Then we are to move with a holy fear in our hearts to build an ark of protection, which today would primarily be a spiritual ark. We must follow His instructions of humbling ourselves, praying, seeking His face, repenting, seeking His righteousness and experiencing revival in our heart. These are His ingredients to build our spiritual ark of protection before the Lord. "If" we do this, we will **be prepared.** His promise is to heal our land (our heart) and provide for our needs.</u>

Isaiah 54:14-17 is a Word from the Lord for those who are willing to make the proper preparation. It states, **"In righteousness you will be established: Tyranny will be far from you; you will have nothing to fear. Terror will be far removed; it will not come near you. If anyone does attack you, it will not be my doing; whoever attacks you will surrender to you. 'See, it is I who created the blacksmith who fans the coals into flame and forges a weapon fit for its work. And it is I who have created the destroyer to work havoc; no weapon forged against you will prevail, and you will refute every tongue that accuses you. This is the heritage of the servants of the Lord, and this is their vindication from me,' declares the Lord."**

IT WILL BE WORTH IT ALL

7

Regardless of what the days ahead may bring, our faithfulness to the Lord Jesus Christ as our Savior and Lord will be worth it all. I am going to shift gears, so to speak, as I finish this book and write you a personal letter of encouragement.

Called by God to serve as an elder and teacher in the body of Christ, I was inspired by the Lord to write this letter to you in our day where sin openly and freely abounds and the growing tendency is to accept many religious beliefs as being in right relationship with God.

Dear Friend:

HAVE YOU EVER WONDERED: "WHO IS GOD?" In deep, wide divergence from the worship of all other deities, Israel worshiped one God alone. He is the Creator of the sun, moon, stars, and all other existing realities, including angels and human beings. He is invisible, absolutely sovereign, utterly holy, all powerful, with unyielding righteousness, yet completely a God of compassion and mercy who enters into a covenant with all mankind who come to Him in faith believing in Him and the teachings of His Word. He is a God to be feared yet loved. He draws near to us, seeking our worship, obedience and fellowship. Scholars have estimated that God is at least 100 million times smarter than man, stating that this would be the minimum intelligence required to create something as complex as humans, along with all of the other living creatures and the environment of the earth and universe necessary to sustain life. God created all things so that mankind could exist as a living being.

The purpose of the Bible, though written by men, is not to propound a philosophy of man. Its concern is exclusively man's relationship to God; not what humans are in themselves, but rather what they mean to their Maker. It conveys the truth that mankind was made for fellowship with God. In contrast with the lower animals, humans have a unique relationship with God.

YOU ARE A SPECIAL CREATION OF GOD! Mankind is a special creation out of a special deliberation of God. **"Then God said, 'Let us make man in our image, in our likeness...'"** (Genesis 1:26). There is nothing like this proclamation elsewhere in the account of the beginnings. Humans were to be special, unique, and different from all other earthly creatures.

Nowhere is there even a hint that this truth applies to the creatures lower than man. That is why God gave mankind "dominion" over all the other creatures. Although humans are similar to other creatures in their physical life, they are not the same in their spiritual nature. Genesis 1:27 says, **"So God created man in his own image..."** That completely distinguishes man from all other creatures. That is why we have intellect, a reasoning power far above all mere animal instinct and intuition.

The mind of an animal cannot reason beyond instinct. The human intellect can reason, know, and grasp realities beyond

Earth, time, and sense; and can contemplate the spiritual, eternal and divine. That is the difference in nature. Those attributes of human intellect are not something which we merely have more of than the lower animals; all creatures other than mankind are absolutely without them.

Humans have a moral consciousness. We are God-conscious beings. We can know God, respond to Him, and commune with Him. The lower animals cannot. The most exhaustive animal psychology has never found the faintest hint of either moral awareness or awareness of a Supreme Being in animals.

You have been uniquely made in the image of God. You are special to Him. You have a special personality unique in all God's creation. He loves you deeply! So much that He literally had His son die for you so He could fulfill His desire to have you spend eternity with Him in a place He has prepared for all His creation, a place called "Heaven."

The Bible knows nothing of extinction—the idea that when the body dies, the human soul also is extinguished. The Bible's teaching of a coming resurrection, and the warning of a coming Judgment Day, all imply that the departed are still alive.

Humans were not meant to die as they now do. We were created to live. And, although mankind fell away from God due to the tragedy of man's sin, the Bible presents God's hope of restoration. It teaches very clearly that when we part from life on Earth, the soul, the spirit of man, the real person continues to live in a place of consciousness.

Paul says that **"...the things which are seen** (here on Earth) **are temporal; but the things which are not seen** (in the beyond) **are eternal"** (II Corinthians 4:18 KJV). It is here on Earth that we are among the short-lived; it is there in the beyond that we will find abiding realities.

Prepare Yourself

When Christian believers die, there is an immediate trans-portation into the Savior's presence, which is to Heaven **"...to be absent from the body is to be present with the Lord"** (II Corinthians 5:8 KJV).

In Heaven, the wonderful bodies we have on Earth will be the same in structure, yet they will be altogether different in texture; instead of being perishable, they will be imperishable.

WONDERING ABOUT HEAVEN

A poll taken of the American people by Market Facts Telenation for *US News & World Report* appeared in the June 20, 1997 edition of *USA TODAY*. It reported *"Adults certain there is a heaven is 67 percent."* Of that number it also reported, *"Adults certain they are going to heaven is 88 percent."* Eighty-eight percent of the adult people in our country who believe there is a Heaven, believe they will go to Heaven.

Why do you think so many people believe they will go to Heaven? It is my opinion, they base their belief on what they hope is true, not what they really know. People don't want to think they are not going to Heaven since this is such an impor-tant issue. It is for eternity. Down deep within, they know that there is a possibility it will either be Heaven or Hell!

In this letter I am going to share some thoughts with you about Heaven[3], as well as Hell[3]. You may agree or disagree with any of my comments. Either way is okay. I have done some research on the subject to share information I believe will bless you. I do not share these comments on Heaven and Hell from an authoritative perspective, as I have never been to ei-ther place. However, I do think the descriptive phrases I share

are in harmony with what the Bible says about Heaven and Hell. Regardless, you must understand these are things reported by man. It is impossible for human beings to be totally accurate because of our limited ability to describe these two places with human language. Heaven is so wonderful, so fantastic, and Hell is so horrible, so awful, that I believe it is actually beyond the human mind to fully comprehend either place.

It is the Lord's desire that every human being goes to Heaven. The Bible was written and has been preserved to show us the way so we won't miss Heaven. I certainly don't want to see anyone miss Heaven. I would never consider spending thousands of hours in teaching and writing if it weren't so important. I have not done it for financial gain, nor do I not take monetary compensation for anything I write or for any of my time teaching. Not that it is wrong to do so, but the Lord has provided for my family's needs through my employment.

I will say it as boldly as I can: You do not want to miss Heaven! Jesus placed a greater value on our going to Heaven than on our gaining the whole world. He knew how important it is. He said, **"What good will it be for a man if he gains the whole world, yet forfeits his soul?..."** (Matthew 16:26). The salvation of one soul is worth more than the value of all the things in the world. But the choice is ours. We must choose between Heaven or Hell. It is a decision all mankind must make while on this Earth. Heaven is a free gift from God, but He has set up some conditions. The conditions are simple. In fact, they are so simple it seems most people pass right over them. My desire is to help people understand why choosing Heaven over Hell is the most critical decision they will ever make in their life. Later in this letter I will review how a person can ensure that they do not miss Heaven.

INTERESTING FACTS ABOUT HEAVEN

In the Bible the words "Heaven," "heavens," and "heavenly" occur 729 times; four hundred thirty-four times in The Old Testament and two hundred ninety-five times in the New Testament. For most people, Heaven means one thing. It is the wonderful place where God centers His presence, where His throne is, where the holy angels are, where the "many mansions" of the "Father's house" are, and where the "redeemed of the Lord" will live in sinless joy forever.

Heaven is a spiritual place for our spiritual bodies, not a material place for our physical bodies. At present we can only attempt to understand Heaven through our physical senses because that is how we identify and define things. The Bible even helps our understanding of Heaven by using descriptive words and phrases of a material nature. This is to help us comprehend Heaven by giving us a more vivid picture of its reality.

Mankind once thought the Earth was the center of the universe. But our sun, with its nine planets and asteroids, is but a dwarf in the particular system to which it belongs. In relation to the whole universe, it is about as large comparatively as a single grain of sand in the Sahara desert.

So immense is the universe in which we live that it has to be measured in "light years." Light, like electricity, travels at a velocity of 186,330 miles per second. One light year is about 6 trillion (6,000,000,000,000) miles. The nearest star to Earth is 25 trillion miles away. There are billions of stars in our universe, and it has been calculated that the cluster of stars in the constellation of Hercules is 36,000 light years away! That is approximately 216,000 trillion miles.

In time, as more powerful telescopes were developed, they not only revealed the vastness of the heavens, but gave mankind the ability to calculate that the universe next to ours contains at least 500 galaxies of its own and is 36,000 trillion miles in diameter. And, there are an infinite number of other universes beyond these.

Where then, is Heaven and the millions of departed Christians? Are they somewhere out there in outer space, millions of miles away from Earth? I don't think so and I will explain why.

Space can be measured. It has dimensions and directions: forward, backward, sideways, and downward. To move from one point to another involves going and coming. The Bible speaks of angels visiting the Earth from Heaven. Such movement takes time. Just as light, speeding through space at 186,330 miles per second takes measurable time, so do heavenly beings, whether with or without physical bodies.

All created personal beings are local, whether an angel, Satan, a demon, or a human being. They can only be in one place at any given instant. If they move from one point to another, it takes time. If Heaven is "light years" away, then it must take "light years" for any created personal being to return to Earth.

Even if they travel at the speed of light, is it practical to think angels reside so far away that it takes them thousands of years of travel to get to Earth from Heaven? Or what about the Apostle Paul whom the Bible says was taken up into Heaven (II Corinthians 12:1-4)? We know it could not have taken a very long period out of his life here on Earth.

There are several indications that Earth, the Lord's initial abiding place for His created beings—mankind, animals, birds, fish—is somewhere near Heaven. Of course, no one can be dogmatic about this subject and can only state his or her personal view. To understand the location of a spiritual place, which Heaven is, is not completely possible with our material thinking minds.

WHAT IS HEAVEN LIKE?

Over the years, various individuals have reported that the Lord has shown them what Heaven is like. I believe some of the reported descriptive accounts of Heaven are worth passing on to you.

The Bible says that a tree is known by its fruit. Therefore, I have only included the accounts of selected individuals after considering how the Lord used these individuals in the Kingdom of God following what they said were visions of Heaven.

For example, John Bunyan was on his way to commit suicide when the Lord gave him His wonderful insights of what Heaven was like. He was then so overwhelmed by the realities of Heaven, he wrote "Pilgrim's Progress," a book which has been used in pointing mankind to the land of realities.

After the Lord let him see the ideal, perfect and glorious utopia of Heaven that he described as exceeding by far the loftiest flights of human imagination, General William Booth became the human instrument of God's power to start the great work of the Salvation Army that still sweeps around the world.

Actually, over the span of the last 2,000 years of the church age, hundreds of individuals from all stages of spiritual development in many different lands, speaking many different languages, separated by decades or centuries of time and who had not communicated with one another, have claimed to have been given divine insights into the realities of Heaven. The amazing thing is those whose fruits confirm they may indeed have had a divine experience, have been in perfect agreement with one another in so many hundreds of details. If these insights of Heaven were not divine, if they were not from one God-given source, disagreement over many countless details would be inevitable.

"No eye has seen, no ear has heard, no mind has conceived what God has prepared for those who love him—

but God has revealed it to us by his Spirit..." (1 Corinthians 2:9,10). I am going to share some insights about Heaven that I believe are worthwhile to consider although it is hard for us to totally grasp the concept of what it would be like living life in the purely spiritual realm of Heaven.

In Heaven humans will experience utter holiness. Jude 24 states, **"...to present you before his glorious presence without fault and with great joy..."** We will reign with Christ in everlasting victory throughout all the ages. Our mental state living in Heaven is so superior to anything known on Earth that words cannot describe it. Mankind will live in a condition of ecstatic joy, so much so that our fragile nervous systems here on Earth could not support such happiness. In Heaven man is immortal. Our capacities are unlimited, supernatural. Our minds and motivations are sinless. Our energy is boundless. This all adds up to joy unspeakable, full of glory. Our cup runs over. Our years never age. We never hunger or thirst any more. God wipes away all tears from our eyes—and never again will we experience any pain, fear, doubt, defeat, regret, misunderstanding, sorrow, or temptation. What utter joy!

Heaven is a place with streets of gold, beautiful streams, trees, flowers, and animal life where we will all have beautiful mansions in the park-like wonders of Heaven's glorious realm. There is no sickness, no pain, no suffering either physical or emotional, and no stress. Everyone lives in complete peace and love in beautiful surroundings, as all provisions are provided for us by a loving God who created mankind and is now caring for all of those who love Him.

This condition will never change. Though we cannot comprehend it, this condition will last for eternity—forever. Everyone in Heaven lives a life full of joy, peace, love and happiness. It will never end.

Prepare Yourself

John Bunyan reported that when he was caught up into Heaven he talked with Elijah, Moses and other Old Testament saints. General Booth stated he saw many patriarchs and many apostles of ancient times and several of the holy martyrs, as well as an army of warriors who had fallen in every part of the world as reported in Scripture. These two men described the wonderful Paradise that exists for all those who are dedicated to serving God. It is a place whose splendor is so magnificent man's language cannot adequately convey it.

After being escorted to the city of God by an angel John Bunyan said, *"Let me stay here, for there is no need of building tabernacles. The heavenly mansions here are ready-fitted."* He also described many different thoughts expressed to him by the prophet Elijah in their conversations. One was the tremendous happiness that exists for all those who are in Heaven.

Elijah expressed it as a complete state of happiness, when the soul and body are completely free of the effects from all sin. As we know, it is the heavy burden of sin that exists here in the world and in our flesh that weighs us down. In Heaven we will be free of the effects of sin, as the bird when it is free of its cage.

Everyone in Heaven receives a perfect spiritual body; the imperfect bodies we used here on Earth have been discarded. And everyone, from the days of Adam and Eve to the present time, is now in this beautiful, wonderful place of Heaven with a perfect spiritual body in which he or she now enjoys blessings that exceed anything ever known on Earth.

After experiencing visions of Heaven and seeing the state of saved man, General Booth attempted to describe the heavenly body, though he declared that it was impossible. In trying to do so, he stated that all disease and all the corroding work of the ages—the physical blemishes resulting from man's fallen state here on Earth—are all done away with in Heaven. Booth said that to describe the shape and features of saints in Heaven was simply not possible, as they are both earthly and yet celestial.

It is beyond words to fully describe from what great depths God has exalted man to such superb heights in Heaven. On Earth, man is weak and sinful, but in Heaven we will appear with grandeur and beauty. We have complete assurance and faith that this is and will be the state of all of those who trust in Jesus Christ for salvation.

The same grandeur has been reported to be true, not only about the spiritual body of mankind in Heaven, but also about the living conditions there. For example, people tell of the indescribable beauty of all the marvels of Paradise, and of all the wonderful mansions. Words failed those who tried to compare the beauty and magnificence of the mansions of the saints to anything here on Earth, even the palaces of nobility! And the same was true of the surrounding conditions in Paradise.

Although the words "gold" and "diamonds" are used in the Bible to attempt to describe items having tremendous value, they fail to come close to the magnificence of the beauty reported to be the condition of the surroundings that await God's people.

Every new arrival will be surrounded by glory so dazzling and overwhelming in every way that their capacity for enjoyment will be filled to the limit; their cup will indeed "runneth over."

Since all of Heaven is a spiritual realm, everything in it is spiritual, and has spiritual values. The parks, the beauty that surrounds each edifice, the animals, the trees, the flowers, the lakes, the rivers, the crystal pools, the shape and size of the mansions, the gems, the jewels—everything contained therein.

Prepare Yourself

Man will be perfected in Heaven. God made human beings in His likeness. The angels who attend, the angels who instruct, the music, the songs, the saints mainly in fellowship, the degree and manifestation of glory, light and life—these and everything else in each park or palace are all working harmoniously for the happiness and joy of the saints. These together all contribute to the spiritual life and development of every saint who dwells therein. There is nothing that does not in some way contribute to the spiritual upbuilding of the life of the saints, or does not help enlarge their capacities for a happier and more exalted life. Everything is one harmonious, progressive, interrelated whole, arranged for the purpose of bringing joy to all the saints who have gone to Heaven—all those who have trusted in Jesus. All who enter this beautiful city will be perfect with the bridegroom, one in love filled with all the fullness of God to live and reign with Him in glory for ages and ages in all eternity (see Ephesians 3:19).

Satan and sin have distorted all the human parts of mankind. However, in Heaven all **five** senses of a Christian, free from all encumbrances, will be perfected. In our youth, the physical senses—taste, smell, sight, hearing, touch—are at their best. In Heaven, the young will have their joy increased ten thousand times, and the old will become young again.

Youth will more than be restored in Heaven; it will be glorified to higher perfection than it was upon Earth. For example, we will have a perfect sense of taste in Heaven that was lost on Earth and which became weaker from childhood on.

In Heaven, unlike on Earth, we do not need to constantly partake of food to maintain existence. Much of our energy on Earth is spent in the search for food and in its preparation. When the Lord placed the perfect man in the perfect Garden of Eden, he was given every herb and tree for food. When man fell, the curse made it necessary for him to eat his bread by the sweat of his brow.

Although much of our earthly enjoyment consists of eating delicious foods, we will partake of Heaven's variety of foods with a more refined sense of appreciation than any human has enjoyed on Earth.

In Heaven, the sense of smell will also be more refined by the perfected order of life. We will have the capacity to appreciate the sweetness of ten thousand perfumes that have been distilled from each flower, filling the whole atmosphere of this beautiful Paradise. This sense will be enlarged beyond all earthly comparison, and we will develop an increasing enjoyment.

Our hearing will be perfected. It has been said, *"All Heaven is an unbroken perfect harmony."* Favorite music and songs that we love to listen to, birds singing that we now hear imperfectly and can only appreciate in part on Earth, will reach heights beyond our imagination in Heaven. In Paradise, because all ears are tuned with God, they are able to hear celestial music beyond the limits of the earthly ear.

Our sight will be perfected. *"Lord, that I might receive my sight"* was one of the appeals of the blind man. How little we see here on Earth. How blind we are to all that is around us! In Heaven, there is no impaired eyesight, no blurred or distorted vision. In God's country, our vision will be limitless in its range. Impaired eyes will be clarified to see all the loveliness and all the beauties of gloryland.

Here on Earth we often pass by thousands of flowers and we don't really see them. There are beautiful birds, animals—all the things of nature—and we often walk right by, seldom giving them a glance.

Even children often joyfully bounce and play around us and go unnoticed, and a hundred other beauties we are too blind to see daily pass our way. Ancient mountains of scenic beauty fail to distract our attention from the path upon which we intently have our minds and eyes fixed. Valleys with rippling hills or plains of daisies excite us very little. It seems as though the powers of darkness make us more blind day by day as we live here on Earth. But in Heaven we will comment, *"Whereas I was blind, now I see."* We will realize that never before have we truly seen beauty in a single lily and will recognize what the Lord meant when He said, **"Consider how the lilies grow...Yet I tell you, not even Solomon in all his splendor was dressed like one of these"** (Luke 12:27).

In the Paradise of Heaven, every flower will be a marvel to us; each petal will be admired. Our eyes will be open to all of Eden's beauty. Not a fir, or a palm, or a moving branch will escape the notice of eyes that God has enabled to sparkle with delight at the beauty to be seen in all the works of His creation. There our eyes will never cease to behold new wonders. Praises will go out to the Lord for every beauty the Savior of mankind has prepared for those who love Him.

Our soul and spirit will be perfected and will be at complete rest. The soul that is never satisfied is at peace. We will be in our heavenly home where our soul shall never hunger or wander anymore. We will know that we have entered a safe haven, resting in perfect peace and complete satisfaction, entirely happy and overflowing with ecstatic joy.

On Earth we have our periods of time—days or hours—or momentary flashes when our minds seem unusually clear. We have times when we are able to think clearly, but in Heaven there will be no faulty memory or confusion of thought, as no imperfection of mind ever falls upon any of God's people in the realms above. Clear thinking, right thinking, deep thinking and divine thinking are the heritage of all who dwell in Heaven.

We will also have perfect knowledge. On Earth, we "see through a glass darkly" at best. That will not be so in Heaven. There will be a wonderful expansion of knowledge and an ability to see things in their right relationships that, on Earth seemed contradictory or unexplainable. Many of the truths of the Bible that puzzle us—truths which the church on Earth divides and splits—will be seen in proper relationship and light. On Earth, our selfish interests are so deep-seated, our preconceived ideas so entrenched, and our personal prejudice so overwhelming in our degenerated and erroneous reasoning power. In his writings the Apostle Paul, the most sincere seeker of truth seems to imply, *"I see through a glass darkly. I know very little. I am picking up pebbles of truth, but every notion of undiscovered truth, what truth I do know, I am unable to fit perfectly into its proper place, in its right proportion and emphasis with all other truths."*

In Heaven we shall be free from all error. We shall be filled with true knowledge to the fullest capacity and we will be gifted with perfect intuition. On Earth, the honeybee knows without being taught how to build a cell that will hold the largest possible amount of honey. This hexagonal cell is of such perfect geometric proportions that man could not improve the plan, and yet the untaught bee—working in unison and perfect cooperation—builds a perfect cell in the dark. This is knowledge without instruction. This is perfect cooperation with a large number of other bees to complete intricate work that puzzles the minds of men.

With this same perfection and in much the same way (perhaps in exactly the same way) God's whole family in Heaven, from lowest to highest, all work together. Each member does his or her particular work, and unseen power from the throne coordinates all the intellectual, emotional and spiritual elements within each individual so that all cooperate perfectly in one great plan.

There is a language in Heaven that all can speak and understand without being taught and there is also knowledge gained without it being consciously acquired. Like the bees in the swarm, each one of us fits into the perfect plan. Each person knows what the other thinks before he speaks. By this heavenly intuition, we will recognize and know everyone in Heaven who were friends or relatives here on Earth. Without even being told, our friends will know of our arrival in Heaven, and they will come to welcome us in the parks or in the mansions. Likewise without introduction, we shall know the patriarchs and saints in Heaven—Abraham, Daniel, Moses, the prophets, and the apostles. We shall know as soon as we see them, and we shall see every one of them. There is in Heaven a higher knowledge than mankind now possesses, and if possessed here on Earth, it is only a fraction of heavenly knowledge.

This intuitive sense we call instinct as it is found in all natural creation, exists in humanly unexplainable terms. The homing pigeon, for example, flies to its home without error. Year after year, the robin returns at the right season to build its nest in the old apple tree. The oriole weaves its hanging nest and knows how to find its food beneath the bark, and where to raise its young in the hollow of the tree. Insects, worms, birds and beasts all know where and how to find the proper food and how to avoid an enemy. Hummingbirds work in pairs in building their minute nest. Ants and bees work in colonies or swarms in perfect cooperation, building geometrically perfect homes. They cooperate in caring for their young and in doing their own perfect bit of life without being taught, without a language or a visible way of communicating thought. They do not think, they do not reason, yet they know. This is but an imperfect illustration of God's great colony or swarm in the everlasting city of Heaven where His knowledge, working in all silent creation, will reach harmonious perfection in everything that exists there—bird, beast and man. Every living creature in Heaven possesses this intuitive knowledge according to his capacity and position in God's economy.

In Heaven, pure love flows like a river from one individual to the next. No one in Heaven can refrain from loving others who are so beautiful and gracious. A perfect spirit pervades all of Heaven where there is no discord, not a rasping voice, not a motion out of rhythm, not an ill-spoken word and not an unkind thought.

In Heaven everyone retains his earthly identity. Love, pure and undefiled, between the heavenly saints in Heaven is more beautiful and thrilling than ever was love between friend, or man and woman. This love, in itself, makes all Heaven a Paradise. This holy love knows no boundaries, and it will never grow cold. In Heaven, love in its highest and purest form is a love that will stand the test of time.

All that mars the best in man is done away with in Heaven. The veil that covers the beauty in each soul is taken away. All are pure, all are perfect. God is love and so is Heaven! There in Heaven all mankind will serve one another. There is no jealousy or even so much as an envious thought. Saints, like angels, are endowed with life from the throne. Everyone helps one another in love without envy or pride. No one will covet another's work; no one will feel his work useless.

Our heavenly homes will be situated where those people we knew and loved on Earth will surround us. We will recognize again the goodness of the Father in allowing friends of the same nationality to be located near each other in Heaven, as on Earth. Everyone will be free of any racial prejudice and pride.

People will be represented from every race, tribe and tongue throughout the Earth. Though each tribe and nationality has its own characteristics, when we meet in Heaven, the love of Christ makes everyone one in heart. Though we may have differences, a common fellowship exists in Heaven making every person feel one with one another. In the Lord, the love bonds between those in Heaven are stronger than the bonds between race and tribe, brother and sister, or father or mother here on Earth.

Another great difference that will exist in Heaven from what we know on Earth is that all work will be done in the fullness and power of the Holy Spirit. Thus, the Holy Spirit filled saints in Heaven will join the angels in never-tiring, never-ending happiness, and will be enjoying their work in the heavenly kingdom of God.

WHAT ABOUT HELL?

The Scriptures confirm that there is also a place called Hell, a place that people try to ignore and really do not want to talk about, think of or comprehend. In fact, the world system has done everything possible to ignore the reality of a place called Hell. The word "Hell" itself has become so commonplace that most often when it is used, the actual terrible reality associated with that word is not even considered. I am going to express some thoughts in accordance with the way I feel the Lord has led me, in order to give you some descriptive phrases and words to help you understand just what the reality of Hell is. In choosing where you will spend eternity—Heaven or Hell—it is important to give strong consideration to the possibility of Hell and exactly what that really means!

In the Gospel of Matthew alone, the Lord warns six times of a place called Gehenna, the final doom of the lost. Actually,

Gehenna was a deep ravine outside the wall of Jerusalem. It was a valley where the city's refuse was dumped and burned, as also were the carcasses of criminals and others. The Lord used it as a symbol of final punishment for the lost so people could clearly understand what His warnings meant.

In Hell, there will be terrible sounds of screaming, pitiful cries and groaning that will fill the air! Noxious odors abound in Hell. There will be great sorrow, pathetic sadness, and horror beyond description.

Let me warn you that there is a place called Hell, and we can be so thankful that God has provided a way so that we do not have to go to that place! It is a horrid place of torment, excruciating pain and eternal sorrow. A person's soul will always be alive in Hell. There will be no joy in Hell, no love, no compassion, no rest—it is a place of sorrow beyond belief.

Fear permeates everything in Hell, with people screaming and trembling with fright. There, the cries of the "living dead" mix with moans and hideous screams, making it impossible for any quiet or peaceful times.

Just as it is in Heaven, in Hell we will still have all of our senses. Sadly, the conditions of Hell are far worse than anyone can contemplate or imagine. And, there is no way out of this torturous place. There is no escape; there is no hope!

It is something like a horror movie where souls are in torment, constant agony and despair. Jesus gave His life so that no one would have to go there. But Satan and all his demons want every person who has ever lived to spend their eternity in Hell. That is why they fight so hard for possession of our soul. That is why they try to deceive us concerning the reality of what the gospel represents and what the love of God has done to save mankind from this place of being lost forever in suffering and pain.

Prepare Yourself

In Hell, the moans, wails, sighs and groans never cease as the souls there are in constant and great torment. The smell of death is constant. Hell is a frightening place of awful sadness and eternal cries of regret.

There will be total darkness in Hell. A tremendous fear grips the soul as it realizes it is lost without hope for eternity. There is no way out so there is a feeling of intense loneliness, utter despair and sorrow enhanced by the ever-present thought of coexistence with demons and evil spirits who torment and constantly bring pain to everyone who dwells there.

Since we are all sinners, and if we have not been saved by the grace of God, pardoned by the acceptance of Jesus Christ as the one who has saved us from Hell, then according to the Bible we are bound to go immediately to a burning Hell—hotter than a lake of fire—when we die. Though the flesh dies, the soul never dies.

The word "Hell" occurs fifty-four times in the Bible; thirty-one times in the Old Testament and twenty-three times in the New Testament. According to Luke 16:19-31, Hell is a place of consciousness. Here the Lord tells us about the "rich man" who died and then awoke in Hell. **"The rich man also died and was buried. In hell, where he was in torment, he looked up and saw Abraham far away, with Lazarus by his side. So he called to him, 'Father Abraham, have pity on me and send Lazarus to dip the tip of his finger in water and cool my tongue, because I am in agony in this fire...send Lazarus to my father's house, for I have five brothers. Let him warn them, so that they will not also come to this place of torment.' Abraham replied, 'They have Moses and the Prophets; let them listen to them'"** (Luke 16:22-24, 27-29).

In these verses the Lord gives us ten different points of evidence that, not only does human consciousness continue in Hell, but it intensifies.

1. **"In hell, where he was in torment, he looked up and saw"**—so he could see.
2. **"Was in torment"**—so he could feel.
3. **"Saw Abraham...with Lazarus"**—so he could recognize.
4. **"He called to him..."**—so he could speak.
5. **"Abraham, have pity..."**—so he could plead.
6. **"I am in agony in this fire"**—so he could suffer.
7. "**Abraham replied** (to him)"—so he could hear.
8. **"Son, remember..."** (verse 25)—so he had memory.
9. **"Send Lazarus to my...brothers"**—so he could reflect.
10. **"So that they will not also come to this place of torment..."**—so he could think ahead.

Hell is terrible! In the New Testament, Jesus gives us grave warnings about this awful place so that we may be stirred to investigate and learn how we may escape the damnation of an existence where "the flame is never quenched."

In Scripture, Jesus comments that there will be gnashing of teeth for those who choose to go to Hell. His life was a message to a lost world that says this: *"I do not desire that you go to Hell."* God made us for His own joy and for everlasting fellowship. We are His creation and He loves us. We can either choose to call upon Jesus and accept Him as our Savior, whereupon He will forgive us and bless us with eternity in Heaven, or we can deny Him.

THE CHOICE IS OURS

We may choose to ignore both Heaven and Hell, and the possible existence of either. Earlier in this letter, I quoted a survey that stated a full 88% of the people questioned who said they believe there is a Heaven, also believe they would be going there. This reasoning is what we want to believe, what we want to hear.

But the God who made the universe, the Earth, and mankind, is the only one who has the position and authority to make that decision. He too, desires that everyone be saved; He wants no one to be lost. But He gave us freedom of choice, so we would not be robots. There are only two places where we will keep on living forever and we will spend eternity in either one place or the other. The choice is ours.

God has revealed this information very plainly through His Word. The message has been made available through writing and through the voices of those who preach and teach from the Bible. We will make a choice in one way or the other. There is no option!

However large and pressing the questions related to our present short life on Earth, they shrink into smallness compared with the subject of death and our vast life hereafter. No matter how wise people may think they are, if they neglect to inquire about the subject of the hereafter, they are fools. Death is a stark reality. It cannot be halted. To act wisely is to face it.

There are millions of people who show little interest, and millions who are deeply concerned but misdirected through untrue teachings and errors about life after death. The Bible—the Word of God—is really the only authority we have. I believe it is the inspired Word of the only true and living God. And, even if you don't agree, I think it is still a source you must at least consider.

Believing that a Supreme Being created the universe and the life in it is easy and sensible. If we just evolved out of matter, how did we develop thought? How did such emotions as love, hate, hope, fear, joy, sorrow, etc., develop out of insensible matter? How did physical atoms and electrical impulses produce a moral conscience in humans? Mind is not mere matter! If we evolved, how did the amazing differences in males and females develop and become so uniquely perfect and able to reproduce life? Or for that matter, why isn't life on Earth now being replenished by more new creatures still evolving rather than by the reproductive system of a male and female?

The soul, that nonmaterial, indefinable substance which is the real you, the real me, outlives all physical change. Even though the body dies, no one has ever seen a soul die. No one has yet been able to supply evidence that the real person, the spiritual soul, actually disintegrates or has given proof that the soul does not live on forever.

A million graveyards tell us that death is man's greatest problem. Death is no respecter of humankind. The words *"Till death do us part"* ring out in every wedding ceremony. Sixty to seventy people per minute pass from this present life on Earth into the life hereafter. The fact that there is life after death is stated in nearly every part of the Bible.

Throughout the Bible there are two choices given to mankind as to where they will spend eternity: HEAVEN OR HELL!

SEARCHING FOR TRUTH THAT LEADS TO HEAVEN

We serve a loving and just God, which the Bible says **"...wants all men to be saved and to come to a knowledge of the truth"** (I Timothy 2:4). As we search for the truth that leads us to Heaven, it is unfortunate that in today's world, there are many types of religions, including different types of Christianity. We need to know the difference between them because only one leads to Heaven and the others do not. Even true biblical Christianity is not necessarily what society presents it to be or, for that matter, what a church may present it to be. The **"knowledge of the truth"** that the Bible is talking about in I Timothy 2:4 is given in the next verse which states, **"For there is one God and one mediator between God and men, the man Christ Jesus"** (I Timothy 2:5).

True Christianity is based on all of the teachings of the Bible—the gospel of Jesus Christ. It is to experience a personal encounter—a personal relationship—with Jesus Christ as Savior and Lord. That is true biblical Christianity! That is the truth that will take you to Heaven.

God's Word states, **"For God so loved the world** (mankind) **that he gave his one and only Son, that whoever believes in him shall not perish but have eternal life. For God did not send his Son into the world to condemn the world, but to save the world through him. Whoever believes in him is not condemned, but whoever does not believe stands condemned already because he has not believed in the name of God's one and only Son"** (John 3:16-18).

"Yet to all who received him, (referring to Jesus Christ) **to those who believed in his name, he gave the right to become children of God—children born not of natural descent, nor of human decision or a husband's will, but born of God"** (John 1:12-13).

Though we may not understand all that happens in the spiritual world, it is when we accept God's Son, Jesus Christ, as our personal Savior that the power of God is released in our lives.

We experience a spiritual rebirth; what is referred to as being "born again." We become a child of the one true God. All children of God will spend eternity with Him in that special place called Heaven that He has prepared for them.

However, there is a second kind of Christianity in the world. I call it the religion of Christianity. There are many people who practice the religion of Christianity, but it is not based upon biblical principles. It directs our faith towards manmade concepts and practices, just like the religion of Israel did when Jesus was here on Earth. A Christian commitment to "things," "doctrines," "ordinances," "traditions," "structures," and "personalities" will not stand the test of true biblical Christian teachings. Our commitment cannot be to something other than Jesus Christ and His teachings as found in the Scriptures. This nonbiblical type of Christianity has caused much confusion. Even more importantly, it has caused people to miss Heaven.

I would never want to point you in the direction of some weak-kneed, shallow Christianity that is not the true way. Heaven is too valuable for that. I am talking about a commitment to something that has more value than gold, silver, diamonds or anything else.

In today's Christian environment it is easy for us to be involved, but that may not mean we are committed to Jesus Christ and His teachings. There is a vast difference. It is very easy to be involved; involvement only means activity. People can be active in a church. Many people are committed to a lot of different things and philosophies. They can even be doing many works in the name of Jesus, but that does not necessarily mean they have experienced a personal relationship with Jesus Christ, and that is what is important. The Apostle Paul was involved full time in the religion of his day, but he said, **"...whatever was to my profit I now consider loss for the sake of Christ.**

What is more, I consider everything a loss compared to the surpassing greatness of knowing Christ Jesus my Lord, for whose sake I have lost all things. I consider them rubbish, that I may gain Christ and be found in Him, not having a righteousness of my own that comes from the law (being able to keep all of the commandments) **but that which is through faith in Christ..."** (Philippians 3:7-9).

Jesus Christ was the true and living God in the flesh, the God who created all things, including you and me. When the virgin Mary gave birth to Jesus, an angel said to the shepherds living out in the fields near His birthplace of Bethlehem, **"'...Do not be afraid. I bring you good news of great joy that will be for all the people. Today in the town of David** (that was Bethlehem) **a Savior has been born to you; he is Christ the Lord. This will be a sign to you: You will find a baby wrapped in cloths and lying in a manger.' Suddenly a great company of the heavenly host appeared with the angel, praising God and saying, 'glory to God in the highest, and on earth peace to men on whom his favor rests'"** (Luke 2:10-14). Jesus became the Savior for all of mankind who come to Him. He will save their souls from Hell. The angels knew how important this was for mankind; it was good news of great joy!

The ministry of Jesus only lasted for about three and one-half years, yet, the effect of His life on the history of mankind has been far greater than that of anyone else whoever lived.

He lived in poverty and was reared in obscurity. He received no formal education and never possessed wealth or widespread influence.

He did not travel extensively. He only once crossed the boundary of the country in which He lived. In infancy He startled a king; in childhood He puzzled doctors; in manhood He ruled the course of nature, walked upon the waves, and hushed the sea to sleep.

He never wrote a book. Yet His life has inspired more books than any other man. He never wrote a song. Yet He has furnished the theme for more songs than all the songwriters combined.

He never gathered an army, nor drafted a soldier, nor used a weapon. Yet no leader ever had more rebels surrender to Him without a shot being fired.

Great statesmen have come and gone. Scientists, philosophers, and theologians are soon forgotten. But the name of this Man abounds more and more.

One day each week, the wheels of commerce cease turning, and multitudes gather to pay homage and respect to Him. His enemies could not destroy Him, and the grave could not hold Him.

Do you know why Jesus has had so much influence? He was God on Earth in the form of a human being. If you want to know God, look at the life of Jesus Christ.

In the Bible Jesus is called: **"The Alpha and the Omega"** (Revelation 1:8); **"Anointed"** (Psalms 2:2); **"Bread of Life"** (John 6:48); **"The Bright and Morning Star"** (Revelation 22:16); **"Chosen and Precious Cornerstone"** (I Peter 2:6); **"Wonderful Counselor"** (Isaiah 9:6); **"Mighty God"** (Isaiah 9:36); **"Deliverer"** (Romans 11:26); **"Emmanuel"** (Isaiah 7:14); **"Eternal Life"** (I John 5:20); **"Firstborn"** (Psalms 89:27); **"Foundation"** (Isaiah 28:16); **"Friend of Sinners"** (Matthew 11:19); **"Good Shepherd"** (John 10:11); **"High Priest"** (Hebrews 4:14); **"I Am"** (John 8:58); **"Our God"** (Isaiah 40:3); **"King of Kings"** (I Timothy 6:15); **"Lamb"** (Revelation 5:12); **"Light of the World"** (John 8:12); **"Living Bread"** (John 6:51); **"Messiah"** (John 1:41); **"Most**

Holy" (Daniel 9:24); **"Physician"** (Matthew 9:12); **"Prince of Peace"** (Isaiah 9:6); **"Rabbi"** (John 1:49); **"Rock"** (I Corinthians 10:4); **"Rose of Sharon"** (Song of Songs 2:1); **"Descended from David"** (II Timothy 2:8); **"Sun of Righteousness"** (Malachi 4:2); **"Teacher"** (John 3:2); **"The Way, The Truth, The Life"** (John 14:6); **"Word"** (John 1:1).

Jesus said, **"...No one comes to the Father except through me"** (John 14:6).

One of the greatest problems we have as human beings in becoming a biblical Christian is that we don't think we can possibly be good enough. Or, we see sin in the lives of Christians which causes us to reject Christian teachings, thinking that can't be the way to God. If that describes your way of thinking, I want to show you **why** that kind of thinking is not accurate. You feel this way because you don't understand true biblical Christianity and what God has done for you.

You are right in thinking that you can't be good enough; no one is good enough for God. You can't pile up brownie points and somehow hope they make you acceptable in God's sight. You don't have to! That is the Good News of the Gospel of Jesus Christ. Our salvation is not based on our being good enough, it is based upon the righteousness of Jesus Christ. This is what the Bible means when it says, **"Salvation is found in no one else, for there is no other name under heaven given to men by which we must be saved"** (Acts 4:12).

Jesus is the only one who was ever good enough to qualify for Heaven. He lived a sinless life! That is how people like you and me are made right with God—that is where we get the righteousness we need. That is why **"Salvation is found in no one else..."** as the above verse states. The righteousness of Jesus Christ is "credited to our account" in the eyes of God when we truly believe in and accept Jesus as our personal Savior. This is Good News!

"**But now a righteousness from God, apart from law** (our keeping all of God's commandments) **has been made known, to which the Law and the Prophets testify.** <u>**This righteousness from God comes through faith in Jesus Christ to all who believe**</u> (accept Him as their Savior – emphasis added). **There is no difference, for all have sinned and fall short of the glory of God, and are justified freely by his grace** (our salvation is a free gift) **through the redemption that came by Christ Jesus. God presented him as a sacrifice of atonement, through faith in his blood..."** (Romans 3:21-25).

God can't pretend sin doesn't exist. He doesn't look at us and make excuses for us. He had to do something about sin to break its power over us. So He sent us His Son Jesus and we have been rescued—redeemed—from Hell by Him. This was accomplished when Jesus died as a sacrifice to pay sin's penalty for all mankind, and to those who believe and receive this offer from God, He does a wonderful thing: He justifies us.

If we need to be justified, it means something is wrong. What is wrong is that we don't match up to the standards of God and God doesn't change His standard in order to justify us. The way the penalty of our sin is taken care of is when we believe in and receive Jesus as our Savior, God does a wonderful thing by applying the righteousness of Jesus Christ to our record. That is how our relationship with God is changed so we fit His standard and can qualify for Heaven—not because we are good enough. **"Know that a man is not justified by observing the law, but by faith in Jesus Christ....because by observing the law** (never sinning by always keeping all of God's commandments) **no one will be justified"** (Galatians 2:16).

Do we deserve this? No, it is God's grace that makes this marvelous gift of salvation from Hell available to us through Jesus Christ. It is a free gift from God. And best of all, it assures us of an eternity in Heaven. How are you going to respond to such a gift? I trust you will receive it thankfully.

The Bible says there is coming a final Judgment Day and that every person will be judged according to the way they lived of their own free will. It says those who are not believers in the gospel of Jesus Christ are condemned. **"Whoever believes in him is not condemned, but whoever does not believe stands condemned already because he has not believed in the name of God's one and only Son"** (John 3:18).

That is a fearful thought! Every human being should stop, listen, and consider while the opportunity lingers. Be done with perilous procrastination. More souls will go to the lake of fire through procrastination than human mathematics can calculate.

I am not just playing on emotions. I am addressing intelligence, conscience, and free will. Death has a way of striking unexpectedly and then the last chance is gone. There is no "second chance." Receive the risen and living Savior Jesus Christ into your heart now. To possess Him is the only way to be eternally saved.

Soon enough all of us must pass over to that other side of the grave. To talk about death is not being morbid; it is just as rational as it is eventually inescapable. For all of us who know the Lord Jesus as our Savior, the grave has been transformed from a foe to a friend. With the backing of the Bible we can say, *"we need have no fear of death."* It will be a wonderful experience. Our last breath here will result in instantaneous complete healing and exquisite joy there on the other side in a better world. Jesus and Heaven are ours! In a word, sunset here is sunrise there! As Paul says, **"For to me, to live is Christ and to die is gain"** (Philippians 1:21).

To the merely natural person, death is the final pauperizing blow; "To die is loss." Nothing bankrupts humans so completely as death. Death is the super-loss, for in that instant, every thrill and ambition is extinguished.

What a contrast is Paul's statement, **"...to die is gain."** Only a Christian like Paul could say it and mean it based on certified guarantees. He knew, as we can now know, how soundly factual is the basis of the Christian faith and hope. Paul actually encountered the risen Jesus on the road to Damascus, and he became a vehicle through which Jesus worked many miracles, even raising the dead.

Paul had searched the sacred Scriptures with scholarly carefulness and had found in them the birth, life, miracles, death, resurrection, and ascension of Christ all clearly foretold centuries in advance through the Hebrew prophets. He knew how true was the fulfillment of those prophecies. That knowledge and more was behind Paul's victory cry, **"...to die is gain."**

There are many reasons why death is gain to those who know Jesus Christ as their Savior. I reviewed several earlier in my discussion about Heaven.

What Heaven represents is unmistakable. To be there will be the highest fulfillment of all pure hopes, ageless vitality and every sorrow healed. Gone forever the burden of mortal flesh and earthly troubles, weakness, pain, temptation, grief, limitation, and frustration. Heaven is a place where there is no unholy thought, desire, fear, doubt, or anxiety. No more hungering and thirsting, every tear wiped away, drinking "living waters" of immortality. It will be a fabulous transition from here to there; from this to that; from now to then. Peter describes it as **"an inheritance incorruptible, and undefiled, and that fadeth not away"** (I Peter 1:4).

All around us will be those shining "clouds of witnesses"— the redeemed of all the centuries, all serving the same Savior and all with pure hearts welcoming our participation. Moses, David, John, Paul, etc., and perhaps Peter himself will interject, **"ye rejoice with joy unspeakable and full of glory"** (I Peter 1:8 KJV).

Added to all that, there will be the reward of reunion with our own departed loved ones who were near and dear to us in this present world. They will be just the same in their physical identities as when they were here with us, except that every wrinkle, every blemish, every disfigurement, every mark of age or weakness will have gone forever. There will be neither any fading of identity nor any blurring of personality. You will always be you. I shall always be me.

A common concern of some is that of what happens to young children who die. The Bible nowhere says or implies that young children who die are lost. Although all who are born are sin-infected, they are not guilty. There is no such thing as inherited guilt. Those who die as children are not saved by their innocence, but they are saved because of it. I believe the Bible teaches that we do not become responsible for our transgressions until we reach a responsible age where we knowingly commit wrong. That, and only that, makes us transgressors and consequently guilty.

Communication, however vivid, cannot properly communicate to any mind limited by sense and time the vastness of all the riches God has in store for those who love Him enough to put their faith in His Son Jesus Christ, the one who gave His life so that all who believe in Him will spend their eternity in that wonderful place called Heaven.

Everyone, however, has a choice to make, and we will choose either Heaven or Hell. Whichever one we choose will be for eternity; it will never end. There are many people who do not want to hear such a statement, but we all will choose one or the other, even if it is by our silence. That is a truth we can't escape regardless of how hard we try.

There are many people who will ignore the reality that they ultimately have to make a choice. They do not want to think about it. There are people who avoid making a choice by convincing themselves that they don't believe in either Heaven or Hell. Or as the poll in *USA TODAY* reports, most people who believe there is a Heaven also believe they will go there. This is their belief without really knowing or trying to find out if there are conditions or requirements. People use these and other rationalizations in order to ease their conscience that they may be making the wrong choice.

If there is **even a possibility** of a Heaven and a Hell, it is far too critical a decision for anyone to pass it off lightly by not thinking about it, by ignoring it, or by not trying to find out all that it involves. That is poor judgment. We are talking about something that is for eternity.

- **You do not want to miss Heaven.**
- **God does not want you to miss Heaven.**
- **I do not want you to miss Heaven.**
- **You do not have to miss Heaven.**

I will again briefly review how we can be sure that we don't miss Heaven. First, we must realize that everyone is a sinner because every person is born with a sinful nature (see Romans 7:14-8:4). By our own life experiences, we know that this is true. Certainly, we would not have wanted to be born with a sinful nature, but the Bible says we had no choice in the matter; it has been handed down to us from our forefather Adam as a part of our nature because of his falling into sin (read Romans 5:12-19). Therefore, none of us—from birth—could ever be good enough to qualify for Heaven. That is why we need a Savior to save us, or our lot would be to spend eternity in Hell. Jesus is mankind's Savior. He accomplished this by coming to Earth and living a sinless life.

God's plan for our salvation is that if we simply believe in and accept His Son Jesus as our Savior, He will credit the sinless life of Jesus to our life, which thus qualifies us for Heaven. That is good news! Mankind has no authority to alter God's plan by using or believing in some other plan that is humanly developed or created.

Is God's plan fair? More than fair! It required great sacrifice on the part of both God the Father and His Son, Jesus. Remember that it has always been mankind who has turned his back on God; God has never turned against mankind. We should be thankful that He loved us enough to provide a plan where we might be saved from spending our eternity in Hell, despite our living contrary to His standards. God didn't have to save us!

CONSIDER THIS

I want you to consider a simple point of logic. If you are a person who believes that you will go to Heaven just because there is such a place and you are right in your belief, it is not going to hurt you to accept Jesus Christ as your Savior as the Bible says you must. However, on the other hand, if you are wrong and the Bible is right, and only those who accept Jesus Christ as their personal Savior go to Heaven, then your choice not to accept Jesus Christ will hurt you for all eternity.

One way of belief has the potential of terrible consequences, the other way, accepting the Gospel of Jesus Christ as presented in the Bible, has no gamble. One choice won't hurt you, regardless of what the truth is; the other choice will cost you your soul in Hell for an eternity if it is not the correct way to believe.

Since our option is to choose one or the other, logically, which is the wise choice? The choice is ours. Like it or not, we will make a choice and it will decide our state of being for eternity. That may sound harsh, but it is the truth. Every person is too valuable to God, regardless of what they may have done in their life up to this point in time. He wants everyone to know the truth. No one could have been any worse than the Apostle Paul before he learned the truth of Jesus Christ.

Repent (decide in your heart to change your way of thinking) and accept Jesus Christ into your heart as your Savior and Lord. That is what Paul did and what millions have done since. It is the only true way to know for sure that you are going to Heaven. If you are sincere and mean it from the heart, you will experience a spiritual rebirth. It is not necessary to understand what all this means. You will know that it happened and you will be in the Kingdom of God and on your way to Heaven.

God knows your heart and is not so concerned with your words as He is with the attitude of your heart. The following is a suggested prayer: *"Lord Jesus, I want to know You personally. Thank You for sacrificing Your life on the cross for my sins. I open the door of my heart and receive You as my Savior and Lord. Thank You for forgiving me of my sins and making it possible for me to spend my eternal life in Heaven. Take control of the throne of my life and make me the kind of person You want me to be."* If this prayer expresses the desire of your heart, pray this prayer right now, and Christ will come into your life as He promised. It is then important that you locate a church that believes in and follows true biblical Christianity so that you can become grounded in the Word of God and be active in Christian fellowship.

Prepare Yourself

The Bible promises eternal life in Heaven to all who receive and remain faithful to Christ. **"And this is the testimony: God has given us eternal life, and this life is in his Son. He who has the Son has life; he who does not have the Son of God does not have life. I write these things to you who believe in the name of the Son of God so that you may know that you have eternal life"** (I John 5:11-13).

Sincerely, I close this letter with God's love,

Bob Fraley

P.S. This chapter seven has also been published in a full color booklet by itself and is available for Christians to share with friends, relatives and church members. The booklet is titled, *It Will be Worth it All.* See Order Form at the end of this book to obtain copies.

References

1. Pat Robertson, "Prepare for Economic Collapse," *End Times News Digest 158* (November, 1991), p. 4.

2. Mark Twain, "Quotable Quotes," *Readers Digest, Vol. 152. No. 911,* (March, 1998), p. 49.

3. This does not reference a direct quote. It references the publications from where many of the thoughts came that I share in describing Heaven and Hell. H. A. Baker, *Heaven and the Angels—4th* edition (Minneapolis, MN: Osterhus Publishing House). J. Sidlow Baxter, *The OTHER SIDE OF DEATH* (Grand Rapids, MI: Kregel Publications, 1987).

135

CHRISTIAN LIFE OUTREACH

The publisher of this book, Christian Life Outreach, is a non-profit (501c3) Christian ministry with several outreach projects that support the body of Christ.

Project—Help the World/Direct: This is a unique inter-denominational ministry where 100% of every dollar donated goes directly to help the poor and needy. All personnel are Christian volunteers who are highly experienced. They offer their services and expertise free of charge. Administrative costs, office expenses, equipment and supplies have also been freely donated. This project is currently helping to meet the needs of people with medicine and health care, famine relief, and church development in Africa and Mexico, along with helping those who are destitute in the United States.

In Kijabe, Kenya, East Africa we are helping in the construction of a major medical training center on the grounds of the African Inland Mission, next to their hospital. We provided the funds for the nursing school girls dormitory and the library, both of which are complete. We have also helped support several health clinics with supplies and facilities that Africa Inland Mission has set-up throughout the country where the trained nurses are sent to provide health care for the native people. By meeting the tremendous health needs among the native people in Kenya they are very open to the gospel of Jesus Christ. Over 50 health clinics have already been set-up and several more are to be added.

Project—Golden Eagle Christian Center: This project is a modern Christian Retreat Center built and operated by Christian Life Outreach near Greenville, Ohio. It serves all Christian denominations. The facility sleeps 64 people and is equipped complete with a commercial kitchen, dining room,

lounge, classrooms, auditorium, gym and other recreation facilities. Contact Christian Life Outreach for a brochure.

Project—Campaign Save America: This project is a
major effort to help Christians understand **why** God's judgment
could fall on America, **what** we can do to prevent it, and **how**
to prepare yourself should it not be averted. The heart of God
speaks a strong message that it is not His desire to bring judgment if it can be avoided as illustrated in the book of Jonah. As
His ambassadors, the responsibility of saving America from
God's judgment is placed directly on the body of Christ. The
mission of Campaign Save America is to help Christians understand what must be done to turn away God's hand of judgment
from falling on our nation (II Chronicles 7:14), and to help Christians prepare spiritually should it not be averted (Hebrews 11:7).

Over 400,000 copies of two different booklets pertaining to
this campaign have been distributed in the last year through
individual Christians and churches from most every Christian
denomination. These two booklets are **free** and will continue to
be distributed at no charge. See the **Book Order Form** at the
end of this book to send for a free copy of these two booklets
and to order other publications pertaining to our current times.

Project—Publishing: Christian Life Outreach helps the
body of Christ stay informed about current events in our changing times through the publishing of books, booklets, and by teaching at churches and Christian gatherings.

For more information about any of our ministries or to re-
quest any of our materials contact Christian Life Outreach,
6438 E. Jenan Dr., Scottsdale, AZ 85254. Phone 480-998-4136.
E-mail: xnlifeout@aol.com or visit our websites at
www.campaignsaveamerica.com
and www.GoldenEagleChristianCenter.org

CHRISTIAN LIFE OUTREACH STATEMENT OF FAITH

1. We believe the Bible to be the only infallible, authoritative Word of God.

2. We believe that there is only one God, eternally existent in three persons: Father, Son and Holy Spirit.

3. We believe in the deity of our Lord Jesus Christ, in His virgin birth, in His sinless life, in His miracles, in His vicarious and atoning death through His shed blood, in His bodily resurrection, in His ascension to the right hand of the Father, and in His personal return to power and glory.

4. We believe that for the salvation of lost and sinful man, regeneration by the Holy Spirit is absolutely essential.

5. We believe in the present ministry of the Holy Spirit, by whose indwelling the Christian is enabled to live a godly life.

6. We believe in the resurrection of both the saved and the lost; they that are saved unto the resurrection of life and they that are lost unto the resurrection of damnation.

7. We believe in the spiritual unity of believers in our Lord Jesus Christ.

ORDER FORM

As part of the ministry of Christian Life Outreach, we are making copies of this book, Prepare Yourself, available for our cost to print, pack, and postage to mail.

BOOKS

Qty	Title		Each	Total
____	Prepare Yourself	1-9 Copies	$2.00	____
		10 or more Copies	$1.00	____
____	Caught In The Web of Deception - Hardback		$16.95	____
____	The Last Days In America		$10.95	____
____	Holy Fear		$9.95	____
____	The Beast of Revelation 13		$8.95	____

BOOKLETS

Qty	Title	Each	Total
____	Could You Be Caught in the Web of Deception	N/C	____
____	Campaign Save America	N/C	____
____	It Will Be Worth it All - minimum order 10	$0.15 ea.	____
____	Wondering About War - minimum order 10	$0.25 ea.	____

Price per book includes
Handling and Postage **TOTAL** ____

NAME _____

ADDRESS _____

CITY_____ STATE _____ ZIP _____

Phone Orders call: 1-602-998-4136 or e-mail: xnlifeout@aol.com

Tear out or copy this page and mail with dollar amount to:
CHRISTIAN LIFE OUTREACH
6438 E. JENAN DR., SCOTTSDALE, AZ 85254.

PLEASE NOTE: CHRISTIAN LIFE OUTREACH IS A 501 (3c) NON-PROFIT MINISTRY. ALL PROCEEDS FROM THE SALE OF THESE BOOKS ARE USED FOR THIS MINISTRY. YOU WILL RECEIVE A TAX DEDUCTIBLE RECEIPT FOR THAT AMOUNT ALLOWED BY THE INTERNAL REVENUE CODE.